gather

Everyday seasonal recipes from a year in our landscapes

Gill Meller

Photography by
Andrew Montgomery

gather | To collect from different places; assemble | To cause to come together; convene | To draw (something or someone) closer to oneself | To harvest or pick

quadrille

For my girls.

Publishing Director: Sarah Lavelle
Creative Director: Helen Lewis
Photographer: Andrew Montgomery
Designer: Miranda Harvey
Food and Props Styling: Gill Meller and Andrew Montgomery
Copy Editor: Judy Barratt
Production: Stephen Lang and Vincent Smith

First published in 2016 by Quadrille Publishing,
Pentagon House, 52–54 Southwark Street, London SE1 1UN
www.quadrille.co.uk
Quadrille is an imprint of Hardie Grant
www.hardiegrant.com.au

Reprinted in 2016 (twice), 2017
10 9 8 7 6 5 4

Text © Gill Meller 2016
Photography © Andrew Montgomery 2016
Design and layout © 2016 Quadrille Publishing
Photographs of the mill interior on p. 149 and of the boar on p. 217
by Andrew Montgomery, courtesy of *Country Living*.

Cataloguing in Publication Data: a catalogue record for this book is
available from the British Library.

ISBN: 978 184949 713 8

Printed in China

notes on the recipes

Unless otherwise specified, use:
Sea salt flakes, preferably Maldon
Medium free-range or organic eggs
Fresh herbs
Medium vegetables
Whole-fat dairy products
Unwaxed lemons
Salted butter

Source organic, free-range
meat whenever you can, and
use fish from sustainable sources.

Oven temperatures are for a fan
assisted oven.

Use metric or imperial
measurements, not a mixture
of the two.

contents

introduction

I've always liked the word 'gather'. It feels hopeful; natural and very human. It's a word that embodies many of the simple things we do every day. As people, we gather in one way or another all the time. It's what we do.

Our early ancestors were known as 'hunter-gatherers'. They thrived on food from the landscapes that surrounded them: nuts and fruits from the ancient woodlands; fish, seafood and sea weeds from the coastline; plants and herbs from the hedgerows and riverbanks; and meat from the forests and fields.

Each landscape provided them with the diverse range of foods they needed to develop strong, healthy family groups. Our early understanding of wild foods (both plants and animals) led to their cultivation and domestication and the growth of agricultural societies as we know them today. Inspite of this, I think we all still harbour that primitive characteristic to gather, as well as a deep connection to the landscapes we live in.

The reality is, we all have to eat. Few of us can go around picking berries and tracking deer. Between checking emails and doing the school run there's no time. That said, we still gather – we still make a considered motion to collect and assemble ingredients: a loaf of bread; fruit from the greengrocer; cheese; a jar of honey. We lift them in our arms and take them home. In many cases we present them to someone and share them.

The way we gather has evolved, and perhaps inevitably our modern ways have meant we've lost a handle on where our food comes from. And our modern way of eating can mean that, quite often, we don't spend enough time together enjoying a meal.

This multilayered word, 'gather', with all its significance and implications, has helped me find a way to make the most of the food that I eat with my family and friends. It's given me a path to tread that makes sense to me as a cook, and it's given me a genuine appreciation for the happiness that sharing food with other people can bring.

My own gatherings release me, for a time, from the four walls of my kitchen. They take me beyond the door of the supermarket, and away from the noise of the cities and towns. I go out into the light and air of the landscapes that surround me, because I believe that sometimes the best way to get great ingredients is by going directly to the source.

I've always been fascinated by the language of our food-producing landscapes through the year. The stop and start of the land's seasonal output intrigues me. The pace of change, the aesthetic of time, of weather and of light. The flood, the ebb, the disparity in the garden from dawn to dusk. The clarity of frost, the haze of the high-summer harvest, the bleak beauty of February in contrast to the breathtaking panoply of autumn's hues. Every time, every year. It's my clock to cook by. For me, landscapes can evoke memories and awaken the senses in the same way food can. A field of barley reminds me of malt, and my father's tobacco. The heady air of wild garlic in a spring woodland goes hand in hand with the prickly sting of green-barbed nettles, and I recall the endless potions, lotions and concoctions I used to simmer up over campfires as a child. Whether or not these early experiments with fire and food formed the bedrock for my love of seasonal cooking is hard to say, but they certainly helped me develop my curiosity about what landscapes could offer at particular times of year.

I remember, one autumn day when I was nine or ten years old, my friend and I picked a couple of handfuls of field mushrooms. We climbed up an old beech tree and made a small fire in the hollow where the big limbs met the trunk. We cooked the mushrooms, smoky and blistered, and we ate them in the branches of the tree. We had no idea whether they were edible! When I eat mushrooms nowadays I always remember this. I am thankful to be alive, but even more thankful for the memory and the connection with the landscape that I made that day.

The majority of our modern landscapes are now managed, and many far more intensively than they should be. But happily there are still places where the ingredients haven't changed much at all. Over the years and throughout my culinary career, I've been fortunate enough to meet and work with many food producers. There are few simpler, more honest ways to support oneself than working with raw and real ingredients in an ethical and sustainable way. These heroes of food production have a perceptive understanding of the environment and a direct responsibility to care for and nurture their landscape and its nature, in all its splendid degrees, in both a respectful and a considered way. They know that we are all the benefactors.

These remarkable people are as much a part of the evening supper I enjoy to cook and eat, as they are part of their own ever-changing seasonal landscape. The fisherman, the sheep farmer, the gardener… these individuals are the soul and sap of any industrious kitchen, the blood and bones behind all those prime cuts in the butchers shop and the colour and crunch behind the salads, herbs and vegetables I've just picked up for the weekend.

This book isn't just about the provenance of ingredients. It's not necessarily about the people who grow, catch, farm, harvest or collect them either. It's not even about the landscapes. It is, more or less, a collection of simple recipes I love to cook, centred on a group of seasonal ingredients of which I'm particularly fond. Through these ingredients I hope to give every home cook an idea of context; a sense of the productive and beautiful places these foods come from. I'm sure many of them are ingredients you spend time preparing in your kitchen, too.

Alongside this, my book is very much about that moment of pleasure when we first taste a dish. That fraction of time given over to the appreciation of all that makes a mouthful of food a joy. It should be this way; joy is, after all, the single most wonderful thing about eating, as pure an emotion as love or fear: the fragility of a perfectly cooked piece of fish as it flakes in the mouth, or the crispness of a fried potato, spiked by the hard edge of rosemary's perfume; the clean, glassy crunch of a fresh lettuce leaf, a lick of lemony acidity its only foil. All these gorgeous textures, tastes and smells are owed in part to the cook's careful and sure hand, but also to the journey the ingredient has made before it hits the plate or the pan or the hot embers of a barbecue.

For me, this way of thinking makes the whole experience of cooking all the more rewarding. In many respects, the act of cooking is simply a culmination, an ingredient's 'last dance', so to speak. Take a bacon sandwich, for example. Turn the clock back four seasons, to the beginning of the journey, and what you've eaten would look very different indeed. It would look like a freshly sown field of wheat and a newly farrowed pink piglet.

If you have an opportunity, go back to the beginning occasionally. Try stopping at a farm gate once in a while, or chatting to the fishermen at the harbourside. Go to a 'pick-your-own' cooperative in June or July. You'll find you nearly always end up with the freshest and most delicious ingredients to cook with; you may even meet the producers themselves. What's more, you'll be able to support them directly and see where your food comes from. I'd also implore you to have a go at gathering a little of your food for free, straight from the hedgerow or the seashore. A simple walk with a basket in hand may well turn out to be a productive adventure, giving you the basis of a satisfying supper.

My respect for and appreciation of good fresh, seasonal ingredients and where they come from have shaped and honed the way I cook. They have taught me to rely more and more on the natural qualities they possess, and helped me to define a style of cooking that is both simple and, for the most part, quick. Mine is an approach that doesn't call for complex processes or tricky techniques. More often than not, my recipes contain just three or four main ingredients combined in such a way as to complement each other without compromise. My ideas are conceived out of a love for simple, but not always typical, combinations. The role of each element within the dish is usually quite obvious, but in many cases will also bring a subtlety and delicacy.

Over the last two decades, I've discovered that cooking with the seasons is not only the best way to enjoy great ingredients in their prime, but also the most creative way to embrace them. It locks me into the patterns of a year like nothing else. I've learned to make the most of what I have in the moment, and to anticipate the new with reverence and desire. In a sense, then, *Gather* has become a philosophy for a more mindful way to cook and to eat.

farm

farm | Tracks and furrows in fields, stamped and shaped. Curved, swept stone forms make standing boundaries. Corrugated sheets on sheets make shelter. Lines in the earth run with water. Thick hedges catch sheep's wool; wellies in the long grass. Cold, damp concrete, stainless parlours and bristle brushes. Troughs, sacks, black tyres, creosote and rusted metal gates, holes in buckets, pig arcs. Spring, first light, magpies, breakfast, honey hives, and warm milk.

cheese

milk

pork

mutton

honey

Blue cheese with honey, thyme, dates, fried onions & seeds

I recall overhearing this conversation between my eldest daughter and my youngest as the two of them were snacking in the kitchen after school. For me, it was a priceless and very sweet little educational exchange about food.

'You know that's mould don't you?' 'No, it's not!' 'What the hell, that's mould; I can't believe you don't know that!' 'It's just blue cheese.' 'No, it's mould!' 'Really?' 'Yes...! 'Oh...'

The funny thing was that the youngest one really loved blue cheese, but she seemed to lose interest after this. Still, I think this fruity salad, with sticky dates and crunchy pumpkin seeds might very well bring her round again.

SERVES 2

2 tablespoons extra-virgin olive oil

1 onion, finely sliced

2 thyme sprigs, leaves picked

1 tablespoon pumpkin seeds

150g (5½oz) blue cheese, such as Harbourne Blue or Perl Las

6–8 Medjool dates, roughly chopped

4 teaspoons runny honey

2 teaspoons cider vinegar

salt and freshly ground black pepper

Place a medium frying pan over a medium heat. Add half the olive oil, then the onion. Cook the onion, turning regularly, until soft and caramelized. Add half the thyme leaves to the onions along with the pumpkin seeds. Toss the onion, pumpkin seeds and thyme together and cook for a further 1 minute, then turn off the heat.

Crumble the cheese over two plates, dividing it equally between them, then do the same with the chopped dates. Divide the warm onion mixture between the two plates, then drizzle over the honey. Roughly tumble each salad together.

In a small bowl, make a dressing by combining the remaining olive oil with the cider vinegar. Season the dressing with salt and pepper, then drizzle it over the two salad servings, scatter over the remaining thyme leaves, and serve immediately.

Curd with radishes, spring onions & herbs

Who wouldn't be into the idea of taking something crisp, like a toasted slice of sourdough or a broken seed-covered cracker, and spreading it thickly with fresh sheep's curd? If someone offered me that, I would think it were almost perfect and I would take it. Add some flaky salt and good olive oil and that's it. This salad, beautifully fresh and simple to assemble, is based on the same notion, pairing a smooth and rich curd with something undeniably crunchy — new season, firm, red radishes. Fresh garden herbs and lemon add a beautiful fragrance.

SERVES 2

12 radishes with their green tops

4 spring onions

2 or 3 mint sprigs, leaves picked

1 small bunch of dill

2 tablespoons extra-virgin olive oil

juice and finely grated zest of 1 lemon

100g (3½oz) fresh sheep's or goat's curd

salt and freshly ground black pepper

Wash the radishes, then give them a quick trim if they need it, removing any tired leaves from the green tops. Using half of them, slice the roots across their circumference into rounds of 1–2mm (¹⁄₁₆–⅛in) thick. Place the radish slices in a bowl, and set aside the tops.

Trim any roots from the spring onions, then thinly slice the white bulbs and most of the green stems at an angle. Add the onion slices to the sliced radish.

Chop half the mint leaves and half the dill and stir them through the radish and onion mixture, along with 1 tablespoon of the olive oil, half the lemon juice and a little of the lemon zest. Season with salt and pepper, then stir again. Cut the remaining radishes in half from root to tip, trying to keep the green leaves attached to each half.

To assemble, place a spoonful of curd on a plate. Arrange half the radish halves and the reserved tops around the plate, then scatter over half the dressed radish and onion mixture. Repeat for a second plate. Tear over the remaining dill, then scatter over the remaining whole mint leaves, olive oil and lemon juice. Season again with salt and pepper, then serve straight away.

Goat's cheese with rhubarb & lovage

Whenever I eat goat's cheese, I am transported back to summer holidays in the south of France, where the hot sun would stale the baguettes by mid-afternoon, and yet they would still seem perfect. I have an indelible image in my mind of an entire table of impeccably displayed, handmade goat's cheeses. They were beautifully finished in flowers and herbs, ash, spice, leaves and seeds. It was the colour, contrast and care their maker had taken over the presentation that I loved so much. I use slices of rinded goat's cheese in this recipe – you can find it anywhere. However, you might have to look a little harder for the wonderfully distinctive herb lovage. It's unbelievably delicious with rhubarb, and works so well with the cheese.

SERVES 4

2 or 3 rhubarb sticks

50g (1¾oz) golden caster sugar

4 or 5 lovage leaves, finely chopped, plus a few whole leaves to serve

4 teaspoons runny honey

4 slices malted bread

1 tablespoon extra-virgin olive oil

200g (7oz) fresh, soft goat's cheese, sliced

salt and freshly ground black pepper

Trim the papery bases from the rhubarb sticks, then gently wash the sticks. Cut each one into 3–4cm (1¼–1½in) pieces and place the pieces in a single layer, if possible, in a large heavy-based pan.

Scatter the sugar and the lovage leaves over the rhubarb, then drizzle over 2 teaspoons of the honey and 2 tablespoons of water. Shake the pan and place on the hob over a low–medium heat. Bring the mixture to a simmer, then cook for 3–4 minutes or until the rhubarb is just beginning to tenderize and the syrup is thickening slightly. Remove the pan from the heat and set aside.

Toast the bread slices on both sides, then place them on a grill pan and drizzle over the olive oil and the remaining honey. Top with an equal number of goat's cheese slices and place the toast under a hot grill for about 4–6 minutes, until the cheese is lightly brown and bubbling. Carefully remove from the grill and place a slice of toast on each of four plates. Top each slice with some of the warm rhubarb mixture, dividing the mixture equally between each slice. Season with salt and pepper, then finish with a scattering of fresh lovage leaves to serve.

Yoghurt & cardamom sorbet with brown butter & poppy seed biscuits

I like the way the cardamom and orange seem somewhat silent in the cold ice of this delicate yoghurt sorbet: they are there – but only just – dancing around the edge with a subtlety that just begins to warm the whiteness. The brown butter biscuits have richness to their crumb and the tiny poppy seeds pop and bite against the smooth sorbet.

SERVES 8–10

FOR THE SORBET
100g (3½oz) golden caster sugar

4 teaspoons runny honey

6 cardamom pods, bruised

pared zest of ¼ orange

600g (1lb 5oz) plain natural yoghurt

FOR THE SHORTBREAD
150g (5½oz) unsalted butter

75g (2½oz) golden caster sugar, plus extra for sprinkling

150g (5½oz) plain flour

75g (2½oz) cornflour

pinch of salt

1 tablespoon poppy seeds

To make the sorbet, place the sugar and honey in a small pan with the cardamom pods, the orange zest and 4 tablespoons of water. Place over a low heat and bring the liquid to a gentle simmer. Cook for 3–4 minutes, or until the syrup begins to thicken slightly. Remove from the heat and set aside to cool.

Put the yoghurt in a mixing bowl. Strain the syrup through a sieve onto the yoghurt and whisk thoroughly. Pour into an ice-cream machine and churn until soft set. Transfer to a plastic container, cover and place in the freezer until frozen (about 3–4 hours or overnight).

To make the shortbread, heat the oven to 170°C/325°F/gas mark 3. Place the butter in a pan over a low–medium heat. Shake the pan once in a while to stop the butter spitting. Cook for about 5–6 minutes, until the butter smells fragrant and nutty and you see the solids browning on the base of the pan. Skim any foamy bubbles from the top. Place the sugar in a bowl, then pour over the butter, leaving the solids in the base of the pan; mix well. Combine the flour, cornflour and salt in a separate bowl, then add to the butter and sugar mixture. Use a spatula to bring everything together to a soft dough. Spread the dough evenly over a non-stick 25 x 15cm (10 x 6in) baking tray, pressing it down with a spatula to level it. Bake in the oven for 15–20 minutes, until golden. Remove from the oven and sprinkle with caster sugar and the poppy seeds. Use a knife to score the biscuit into rectangular fingers. Allow to cool.

Remove the sorbet from the freezer 15 minutes before serving it – a spoonful per person with a crumbly biscuit alongside.

Crème caramel with vanilla & anise

Every time I taste a good crème caramel, I become a little fonder of this easy-to-make milk pudding. I love its texture and the way you can almost cut it. My mum makes a birthday crème caramel for my dad; it's his favourite. Last year's was a particular triumph, with the smoothest texture of all her crème caramels to date. We put this down to the fact that her electric whisk had broken, so she had to incorporate the eggs into the hot milk and cream with a fork instead.

SERVES 6

200g (7oz) golden caster sugar

250ml (9fl oz) whole milk

250ml (9fl oz) double cream, plus extra for serving

1 vanilla pod

2 star anise

2 large eggs, plus 3 yolks

To make the caramel, place a large, heavy-based pan over a low heat. Add 150g (5½oz) of the sugar, and allow it to melt gradually. Try not to stir it too much, as it can begin to crystallize – the occasional shake and swirl will help things along, though. As soon as it's melted evenly and looking golden, remove it from the heat. Pour the caramel into a heatproof dish roughly 25cm (10in) across and 5cm (2in) deep, or into 6 individual ramekins, then leave to set.

Heat the oven to 150°C/300°F/gas mark 2. To make the custard, place the milk and cream in a large pan. Scrape the seeds from the vanilla pod and add them with the star anise to the milk and cream, along with the pod itself. Place the pan over a medium heat. As soon as the mixture begins to simmer, remove the pan from the heat and allow the creamy mixture to infuse for 10 minutes.

Crack the whole eggs into a large bowl, then add the yolks and remaining sugar. Gradually pour the warm milk mixture into the eggs and sugar, using a fork to beat together as you go. Strain the mixture through a sieve into a jug, then pour it over the caramel.

Place the dish or ramekins into a roasting tray. Pour boiling water into the tray until it comes halfway up the sides of the dish or ramekins. Place in the oven and bake for 45 minutes for one large dish or 18–20 minutes for ramekins, or until the custard is just set with a bit of a wobble. Remove from the oven, cool, then refrigerate. Remove from the fridge 30 minutes before serving. When ready to serve, run a sharp knife around the rim to release the edge of the custard. Place a large plate over the top (or individual plates over each ramekin), then carefully invert so that the pudding pops out onto the plate. Serve with cream, and cooked plums if they're in season.

Homemade cheese with herbs, lemon & olive oil

I like the alchemy involved in this simple homemade cheese. One moment it's a pan of white liquid as pourable as water; the next, it's a singular, solidified mass. You can't see the precise moment of magic: the milk sets, but you never see it happen, even if you look really closely. You have to lift the delicate curds from the whey and allow them to drain (you'll need a large square of muslin or cheesecloth for this). Keep the whey, though – it's good for making bread, soups and smoothies. I've even made sorbet with it.

MAKES 500G (1LB 2OZ)

1.2 litres (40fl oz) whole milk

1 teaspoon vegetarian rennet

2 tablespoons plain natural yoghurt

1 bunch of mixed herbs, such as dill, fennel tops, parsley, chives and sage, roughly chopped

finely grated zest of 1 lemon

1 teaspoon chilli flakes (optional)

extra-virgin olive oil, for drizzling

salt and freshly ground black pepper

Place the milk in a large pan over a low heat. Heat to hand-hot, then turn off the heat. Add the rennet and the yoghurt to the milk, whisk to combine, then set aside for 25–30 minutes until the curd has formed.

Using a sharp knife, cut the curd in a criss-cross pattern and leave for a further 25–30 minutes. Then, very carefully, use a slotted spoon to lift the curds from the whey. Place them straight into a muslin-lined sieve set over a bowl and transfer everything to the fridge for 8–12 hours or overnight, allowing the curds to drain.

When you're ready to serve, remove the sieve from the bowl and turn the curds out onto a large plate or into a bowl. Season well with salt and pepper. Scatter the chopped herbs over the cheese, along with the lemon zest, and the chilli flakes, if using. Finish with a generous drizzling of extra-virgin olive oil (the best you can find) and bring the whole thing to the table. Eat with hunks of good bread, or maybe some roasted vegetables or grilled lamb.

Roast pork with herbs, broad bean tops & new potatoes

Roast pork belly with crackling would be on the table of my last supper – I love it. It's to do with the balance of textures: the salted crunch of the brittle, puffed rind, the meltingly tender open grain of the meat, and the creamy, almost buttery nature of the soft white fat. It's so deeply savoury and so sedately satisfying to me, I can imagine falling quite happily into a big sleep. This recipe is a little different from a typical roast. Simple boiled new potatoes and fresh broad-bean tops, with lots of herbs and lemon, perfectly balance the rich meat. Buy the best pork you can: free-range or organic pork, particularly from rare or traditional breeds of pig, will be much more delicious and characterful.

SERVES 4

3–4 teaspoons fennel seeds

1.5kg (3lb 5oz) thick end of pork belly, bone in, skin completely dry

300g (10½oz) new potatoes

3 or 4 mint sprigs, leaves picked and finely chopped, stalks reserved

1 knob of butter

2 tablespoons extra-virgin olive oil

1 small bunch of parsley, leaves picked and finely chopped

1 small bunch of chives, finely chopped

2 handfuls of broad bean or pea tops, plus any flowers if available

juice of ½ lemon

salt and freshly ground black pepper

Heat the oven to 220°C/425°F/gas mark 7. Toast the fennel seeds in a small pan over a medium heat until fragrant. Remove from the heat, then use a pestle to grind them coarsely in the pan. Use a sharp knife to score the skin and fat of the pork (don't cut into the meat). Place the pork in a roasting tray and rub all over with salt and the crushed fennel. Place in the oven for 25–30 minutes, then reduce the heat to 160°C/315°F/gas mark 2–3, add half a glass of water to the tray, and roast for 2 hours, until golden, tender and giving. (Add a splash more water if at any time the pan looks dry.)

While the pork is roasting, halve the new potatoes if they're large and place them in a pan along with the reserved mint stalks. Cover with well-salted water and simmer for 8–15 minutes (cooking time will vary according to how fresh your potatoes are and the variety), or until just tender, then drain and return to the pan, discarding the mint stalks. Add the butter and 1 tablespoon of olive oil, season well with salt and pepper, stir together, then set aside.

Once cooked, remove the pork from the oven and rest it for 15–20 minutes. Add the fresh herbs to the potatoes, stir through, then spoon the potatoes onto a warm platter. Place the pork on the platter, then skim off the fat from the juices in the roasting tray and spoon the juices over the pork and potatoes. Place the broad bean or pea tops in a bowl, dress with the remaining olive oil and the lemon juice, and season with salt and pepper. Stir, then scatter over the pork and take to the table straight away.

Bacon with cuttlefish, lemon, tomato & bay

This is the sort of dish I really like to cook, but also long to eat. It's forcefully rich, moody and sweet, and crushingly delicious. It's a dish that slows down time. I like the way these two robust ingredients, cuttlefish and bacon, submit to the low heat of the oven. They yield and tenderize at the same reluctant rate; they both add, neither subtracts. Pearl-white cuttlefish has a very unique flavour when slow-cooked in this way. If you haven't had it before, I'd urge you to have a taste.

SERVES 4

1–2 tablespoons extra-virgin olive oil

1 x 400g (14oz)-piece skin-on bacon or pancetta, cut into 4 equal pieces

1 cuttlefish (about 800g–1kg/1lb 12oz–2lb 4oz), ready to cook; ink reserved, if available

1 large onion, thinly sliced

2 garlic cloves, peeled and thinly sliced

1 teaspoon fennel seeds

pared zest of ½ lemon

2 bay leaves

½ glass of white wine

200g (7oz) tinned tomatoes

400ml (14fl oz) pork or chicken stock

salt and freshly ground black pepper

Heat the oven to 160°C/315°F/gas mark 2–3. Heat a dash of olive oil in a medium frying pan over a medium–high heat. Place the bacon pieces in the pan and cook them on each side until golden and starting to caramelize (about 8–10 minutes). Remove from the heat and set aside.

Using a sharp knife, cut the cuttlefish body into strips of about 2–3cm (¾–1¼in) wide. Cut the tentacles into small pieces. Return the bacon pan to a high heat and add all the cuttlefish pieces. Fry, turning occasionally, for 5–6 minutes, or until the fish pieces take on some colour.

Meanwhile, heat 1 tablespoon of the olive oil in a large heavy-based casserole on a medium heat. Add the onion and garlic and cook for 4–5 minutes, until the onion is beginning to soften. Add the fennel seeds, lemon zest and bay leaves. Cook for a further 2 minutes, then add the wine. Bring to a simmer, reducing the liquid for 1–2 minutes, then add the tomatoes and the stock, and return to a gentle simmer. Add the bacon and cuttlefish and stir to combine. Make sure the bacon is just submerged in the sauce.

Put a lid on the casserole and place it in the oven for 2–3 hours, or until the bacon is tender and giving, and the cuttlefish is soft. Remove the casserole from the oven, lift the lid and give the bacon and cuttlefish a stir. Taste and adjust the seasoning, if necessary. If you have the cuttlefish ink you can stir it in at this point – it will darken the sauce and enrich the dish. Serve straight away with hunks of good bread and a crisp salad.

Black pudding with sage, onions & duck eggs

You don't have to make your own black pudding to enjoy this one-pan breakfast or supper – you can buy really good organic black pudding, which is sweet and full of flavour, easily these days. However, if you're up for it, making your own is great fun and not at all grisly. This recipe makes enough for two loaves altogether, which is more than you'll need for one breakfast.

SERVES 2

1 small knob of butter

1 tablespoon extra-virgin olive oil

1 onion, very finely sliced

250g (9oz) black pudding (see below)

12 sage leaves

2 duck eggs

2 or 3 thyme sprigs

salt and black pepper

FOR THE BLACK PUDDING
(MAKES 2 TERRINES)

500g (14oz) pork back fat

4 onions, diced

2 teaspoons ground black pepper

2 teaspoons ground coriander

½ teaspoon ground mace

½ teaspoon hot smoked paprika

20g (¾oz) soft brown sugar

4 teaspoons salt

100ml (3½fl oz) double cream

100ml (3½fl oz) brandy

1 litre (35fl oz) pig's blood

250g (9oz) fine oatmeal

200g (7oz) breadcrumbs

250g (9oz) cooked pearl barley

To make your own black pudding, heat the oven to 120°C/235°F/ gas mark 1. Place a large, heavy-based pan on a low heat. Dice the pork fat, add a quarter of it to the pan and cook, stirring, until it starts to render. Add the diced onion and cook for 8–10 minutes, until soft but not coloured. Remove from the heat, then add the remaining fat along with all the ground spices, and the sugar and salt. Stir to combine. Pour in the cream and brandy, then, once the pan has cooled a little, slowly add the blood, stirring continuously. Fold in the oatmeal, breadcrumbs and pearl barley and let stand for 30 minutes to thicken a little.

Line two 450g (1lb) loaf tins with cling film, leaving some excess overhanging. Stir the mixture, then divide evenly between the tins. Fold the overhanging cling film over the top. Cover with foil, crimping it tightly around the edges. Place the tins in a roasting tray half filled with hot water, then place the whole lot into the oven and cook for 1½ hours, or until the internal temperature of the pudding reaches 72°C (162°F; you'll need a probe for this). Allow the puddings to cool before turning them out and refrigerating.

To make the dish, melt the butter with the oil in a large frying pan over a medium heat. When it's bubbling, add the sliced onion and season. Cook, stirring regularly, until the onion starts to crisp at the edges. Remove onto a plate and keep warm. Slice 250g (9oz) black pudding into 1–2cm (½–¾in) slices and add to the frying pan. Tear in the sage leaves. Fry the pudding slices for 3–4 minutes on each side, until crisp. Return the onion to the pan to heat through, then use a spatula to move the black pudding to the side of the pan. Crack the duck eggs into the pan. Season, and scatter over some thyme leaves. Cook the eggs to your liking. Serve the black pudding on plates with the onions and sage, and the eggs alongside.

Fried mutton loin with shaved cauliflower, preserved lemon & smoked paprika

I remember being told the best thing to do with an old mutton carcass was to 'slow-cook the whole thing'. I was younger and less experienced, but we had hung that thing for four weeks. The meat was dark and dry and carried a good-looking, firm, white fat. I kind of hoped the loins would be tender enough to serve pink. So, ignoring the slow-cooking advice and without really knowing how things would turn out, I cooked the loins hot and fast, with coarse salt, olive oil and the verve of youth. The meat was sensational — as tender as you could wish for.

SERVES 4

1 small, firm cauliflower

6 tablespoons extra-virgin olive oil

juice of ½ lemon

2 teaspoons cumin seeds, toasted

2 or 3 mint sprigs, leaves picked and shredded

1 tablespoon pumpkin seeds

2–3 teaspoons sunflower seeds

1 large or 2 small white onions, thinly sliced

250g (9oz) mutton loin, trimmed

1 garlic clove, bashed

skin of 1 small preserved lemon, very thinly sliced

1 tablespoon runny honey

1½ teaspoons sweet smoked paprika

6–8 sprigs fennel tops, torn

salt and freshly ground black pepper

Cut away the outer leaves from the cauliflower, then trim back and remove the central stem, dividing the cauliflower into large florets as you do so. Thinly slice the florets about 2–3mm (¹⁄₁₆–⅛in) thick and place them in a large bowl. Drizzle over 2 tablespoons of the olive oil, pour over the lemon juice and scatter over the cumin seeds and mint leaves, then season well with salt and pepper. Use your hands to tumble everything together gently and set aside.

Set a large frying pan over a medium heat and add a dash of olive oil, followed by the pumpkin and sunflower seeds and a scattering of salt. Toast the seeds for 3–4 minutes, then remove them from the pan and set aside. Return the pan to the heat, add a further 2 tablespoons of olive oil and when the oil is hot, add the sliced onion. Season, then cook, stirring regularly, until the onion is soft and beginning to crisp around the edges (about 10–12 minutes). Remove the onions to a plate and keep warm. Return the pan to a high heat. Add the mutton loin and garlic to the pan. Season all over with salt and pepper. Cook for 5–7 minutes, turning regularly, until they've taken on some golden colour, then remove from the heat and allow to rest for 5–10 minutes in a warm place.

Scatter the cauliflower over four large plates or a serving platter. Slice the mutton into 1–2cm (½–¾in) slices and lay it over the top of the cauli. Scatter over the onions and the toasted seeds along with the preserved lemon skin. Drizzle with the honey, and dust with smoked paprika. Finish with a tangle of torn fennel tops, a lick more olive oil and some salt and ground black pepper.

Mutton tartare with pan-roasted oysters & wild garlic flowers

I first made this dish on the beautiful Isle of Sark, off the craggy coastline of northern France. The mutton I used grazed on the green pasture that I could see from the kitchen window. The oysters were fresh, round, briny and effortlessly delicious. Mutton tends to be roasted or braised and oysters are served glamorously raw – here, I've skewed the conventions a little.

SERVES 2

sunflower oil, for deep frying

2 or 3 stems wild garlic flowers

1 tablespoon plain flour

1 tablespoon cornflour

1–2 tablespoons extra-virgin olive oil

1 large knob of butter

2 thyme sprigs

12 large oysters, shucked (see p. 54), liquor reserved

150g (5½oz) mutton loin, well trimmed

juice of ½ lemon

salt and freshly ground black pepper

Place a medium saucepan on a medium–high heat. Pour in sunflower oil to a depth of 3–4cm (1¼–1½in) and bring it up to a frying temp of 165°C/330°F (if you don't have a kitchen thermometer, drop in a cube of bread – if it sizzles the oil is ready).

Wash the wild garlic flowers and shake dry. To make the batter, combine the flour and cornflour in a bowl, season with salt and pepper, then add 3 tablespoons of water and whisk well to combine. Dip the flowers into the batter to coat, then drop them into the hot oil. As soon as they are lightly coloured and crisp (about 45 seconds), remove with tongs and drain on kitchen paper. Turn off the heat.

Place a medium non-stick frying pan on a low–medium heat. Add a dash of olive oil and the butter and, when bubbling, add the thyme springs, then the oysters and their liquor. Cook the oysters for 5–6 minutes on each side, until they are dark and crisp, then turn off the heat. The liquor will have become deeply flavoured – scrape this up from the base but leave it in the pan with the oysters to keep warm.

Trim any outer sinew, fat or aged membrane from the mutton loin to reveal the clean meat. Cut into thin slices, and then finely chop into 2–3mm (1/16–1/8in) pieces. Place the loin pieces in a bowl and season with salt and pepper, then drizzle over 1 tablespoon of your best extra-virgin olive oil and the lemon juice. Taste and adjust the seasoning, if required. To serve, divide the mutton tartare between two plates, put the oysters back on a low heat to warm through and then serve straight away next to the mutton, along with any buttery bits from the pan and the crisp wild garlic flowers.

Slow-roast mutton shoulder with garden herbs

For this recipe you'll need a place to gather; at least half a dozen kind people; six or seven slow, lazy hours, and the heat from a low stove; a table, simply laid; two or three bottles of honest, interesting wine; the capacity to share, down to the bone; hands to hold, bread to break and a spoon to serve the meat. Everything else is just garden herbs and mutton.

SERVES 8–10

1 mutton shoulder, bone in
(about 3–4kg/6½–9lb)

2 tablespoons extra-virgin
olive oil

1 bunch of mixed herbs,
such as rosemary, sage,
tarragon, thyme, bay leaves,
marjoram, fennel tops

2 garlic bulbs, halved
around their circumference

1 glass of cider

1 heaped tablespoon plain
flour

300ml (10½fl oz) vegetable,
chicken or lamb stock

2 teaspoons fruit jelly, such
as redcurrant or crab apple

salt and freshly ground
black pepper

Heat the oven to 200°C/400°F/gas mark 6. Place the mutton shoulder in a large roasting tray and rub all over with the olive oil. Season generously with salt and pepper and place it in the hot oven for 35–40 minutes, until the meat has taken on some colour and is already smelling delicious. Remove the tray from the oven and add the whole herbs, the halved garlic bulbs and the cider. Cover the joint with baking parchment, then the whole tray with foil, crimping it tightly around the edges to keep in the steam.

Turn down the heat to 120°C/235°F/gas mark 1 and return the mutton to the oven. Cook for 6 hours, until the meat is really tender and giving. Then remove the tray from the oven and leave the meat to stand for 20–25 minutes before removing the foil and parchment. Carefully lift the mutton from the tray to a wooden board or a platter.

Use a large spoon to skim off the excess fat from the roasting juices and lift out any remaining whole herbs so that you can use the juices to make a simple gravy. Set the tray over a low heat, add the plain flour and, using a wooden spoon or spatula, work it into the remaining herbs and soft, roasted garlic, scratching free any caramelized sticky bits from the base of the tray. Add the stock and the fruit jelly, stir, then bring up to a simmer and cook for a few minutes to thicken it. Pass the contents of the tray through a sieve into a clean saucepan and bring back to a simmer before adjusting the seasoning to taste. Serve the mutton with the gravy and some simple seasonal vegetables.

Honey cake with coriander seed, spelt & orange

There is something about a sticky, honey-drenched cake like this one that is so appealing, so hard to resist. This cake is made with spelt flour, ground from a very old species of wheat that has a nutty, sweet flavour. Orange zest brings warm citrus, and oily almonds give moisture. But the big players here are the coriander seeds and the honey, which together give the cake not only texture and warmth, but also a deep floral sweetness that will vary from honey to honey.

MAKES 1 x 18CM (7IN) CAKE

275g (9¾oz) butter

250g (9oz) golden caster sugar

4 tablespoons runny honey

grated zest of 1 orange

2 teaspoons coriander seeds, toasted and crushed

4 large eggs

150g (5½oz) spelt flour

2 teaspoons baking powder

150g (5½oz) ground almonds

FOR THE HONEY CORIANDER SYRUP

4 tablespoons runny honey

2 teaspoons coriander seeds, toasted and crushed

juice of 1 orange

Heat the oven to 170°C/325°F/gas mark 3. In a large mixing bowl, beat the butter until creamy. Add the sugar, honey, orange zest and coriander seeds and beat thoroughly until very light and fluffy. Add the eggs one at a time, adding a spoonful of the flour with each and beating thoroughly before adding the next egg and spoon of flour.

Combine the remaining flour with the baking powder and sift into the beaten butter, sugar and egg. Using a large metal spoon, carefully fold the flour and baking powder into the mixture, until combined. Stir in the almonds, and mix until evenly combined.

Grease an 18cm (7in) springform cake tin, then line it with baking parchment. Spoon the mixture into the tin, spreading the cake batter evenly with the back of the spoon. Stand the tin on a baking sheet (the batter may leak a little during cooking) and bake the cake in the oven for about 50 minutes, until the sponge is springy to the touch and a skewer inserted into the middle comes out clean.

Remove the cake from the oven and let it cool slightly while you make the syrup. Combine all the syrup ingredients in a pan, whisk together and place over a medium–high heat, without stirring, for 4–5 minutes, until reduced. Without removing the cake from the tin, gently prick the surface with a toothpick, and drizzle over the syrup so that it soaks into the hot sponge. Leave the cake in the tin for a further 30 minutes or so, before removing from the tin and placing on to a wire rack to cool completely.

The cake tastes best if you leave it for a day or two before eating, and it will store well for at least a week in an airtight tin.

Honey-roast seeds with chilli, thyme & rosemary

How can I argue with honey? It is pure to the point of perfection. A million things with wings have made it. Honey, in all its guises, will always amaze me; it has to be one of my most treasured ingredients. In this recipe it brings sweetness, depth and character to the mixed, toasted seeds. Serve the result with drinks before dinner, in packed lunches, scattered over salads, or as a simple snack on the go.

MAKES 2 JARS

100g (3½oz) pumpkin seeds

50g (1¾oz) linseeds

50g (1¾oz) sunflower seeds

25g (1oz) sesame seeds

4–6 rosemary sprigs, leaves picked

1–2 teaspoons chilli flakes

2 tablespoons tamari or soy sauce

2 tablespoons runny honey

Heat the oven to 170°C/325°F/gas mark 3. Place all the seeds in a bowl. Tear over the rosemary leaves, add the chilli flakes and tamari or soy sauce and toss everything together well.

Spread the seed mixture out over a large, flat baking tray. Drizzle over the honey as evenly as you can, then place the tray in the oven. Bake, turning with a spatula 2 or 3 times, for 12−15 minutes, until fragrant and looking toasty.

Remove the tray from the oven and allow to cool, again turning the seed mixture several times during cooling. The seeds should cluster up a little as they are turned.

Serve straight away, or cool thoroughly and store in an airtight jar or container for 2−3 months.

Spring cabbage salad
with honey & sprouted lentils

This salad is all about the crunch and bite of the raw, and the honey-sweet warmth of the punchy dressing that brings it all together. I always look out for a firm, pointy spring cabbage like the hispi, which is refreshing and crisp. You can pick up sprouted lentils and beans or 'mixed sprouts' in most supermarkets. They are moist, super-healthy and packed with an iron flavour that goes beautifully with the 'spike' of the dressing. Once you have everything to hand, this salad comes together in minutes, making a perfect quick lunch or light supper.

SERVES 4–6

1 firm hispi cabbage
(about 400g/14oz)

4 white or red spring
onions, thinly sliced

150g (5½oz) mixed sprouted
lentils and/or beans

2–3 teaspoons sesame
seeds, toasted

FOR THE DRESSING

20g (¾oz) ginger root,
peeled and finely grated

1 garlic clove, peeled and
finely grated

juice and finely grated zest
of ½ orange

2 tablespoons tamari or soy
sauce

1–2 teaspoons dried chilli
flakes

50g (1¾oz) runny honey

2 teaspoons coriander
seeds, toasted and crushed

2 teaspoons sesame oil

To make the dressing, combine the ginger, garlic, orange juice and zest, tamari or soy sauce, chilli flakes, honey, coriander seeds and sesame oil in a small bowl and whisk to combine. Set aside.

Trim off any rough or discoloured outer leaves from the cabbage. Slice in half from top to bottom, then remove the thickest part of the stem from within each half. Slice each half into thin ribbons, no thicker than 1cm (½in) wide. Wash the shredded cabbage and drain well. You can spin it dry briefly if you have a salad spinner.

Scatter the cabbage over a large serving platter, or onto smaller individual plates. Spoon half the dressing over the cabbage, then scatter over the spring onion.

Place the sprouted lentils and/or beans in a small bowl. Drizzle over 3 tablespoons of the dressing, and tumble everything together. Scatter the lentils and/or beans over the plated cabbage and spring onions. Scatter over the toasted sesame seeds and finish by drizzling over the remaining dressing. Serve immediately.

seashore

seashore | Tangles in glass pools, little feet daring. Lifting rocks, wet socks, the arc of the tideline. Spring's water sculptures in drifting wood, twine loops and plastic colours. Cuttle bones, beach combs and the secret creep of the estuary. Campfires, the spit, the crack of hot flint. My old pans, supper, plans for a night swim. The collector, the deep green and the browns of the waters' weed. White angry barrels, the fall, the push, the suck and drag. Crabs, litter, lobster pots. Mud slips, green tips, marine sky for ever, samphire and the drink.

crab

oysters

seaweed

wild sea greens

mussels

Spider crab with loganberries, lemon zest & fennel tops

When a raspberry falls in love with a blackberry sooner or later you get a loganberry. They are floral and scented; ruby red, juicy and sharp to a point. It's the acidity that I like, which goes so well with the sweet, tender meat of the spider crab – very much as tomatoes do, only fruitier. This fresh combination gets a little bump from lemon zest, and cool, green notes from aniseedy fennel tops. If you can't find spider crab, you could make the dish with the meat from brown crab or velvet swimming crabs.

SERVES 2

200g (7oz) freshly picked spider crab white meat, and brown (optional)

1 small punnet of ripe loganberries or raspberries (about 100g/3½oz)

a few roughly torn fennel tops

a few fennel flowers, if available

2 tablespoons extra-virgin olive oil

juice of ½ small lemon

salt and freshly ground black pepper

Pick over the crab meat to make sure there are no traces of shell. On a large serving platter, or over two individual plates, scatter over the fresh white crab meat and dot over the brown meat, if using.

Roughly chop the loganberries or raspberries in half, and place them in and around the crab meat. Scatter over the fennel tops and the flowers (if using), drizzle over the olive oil and lemon juice, and season with salt and black pepper.

Bring to the table with freshly toasted sourdough to serve.

A crab soup

I've been making this soup for years, nearly always the same way and never from a recipe. It's so unbelievably good that I thought I'd better note down all the things I put in it. Essentially, it begins with crab and ends with crab. But then there's cream and thyme and cider brandy…

SERVES 4–6

1 tablespoon extra-virgin olive oil

1 large knob of butter

1 onion, chopped

1 small fennel bulb, trimmed and chopped

1 carrot, peeled and diced

2 celery sticks, chopped

2 garlic cloves, grated

1 bay leaf

2 thyme sprigs

1 good-sized tarragon sprig

1 teaspoon paprika

1 teaspoon fennel seeds

1 small star anise

½ glass white wine

250g (9oz) tomatoes, skinned and chopped, or 250g (9oz) tinned chopped tomatoes

1.2 litres (2 pints) crab stock

75ml (2¼fl oz) double cream

1 small glass of cider brandy

salt and black pepper

FOR THE CRAB STOCK

2 picked brown or spider crab shells, including legs and body

2 fresh flat-fish frames (skeletons)

1 onion, thinly sliced

2 celery sticks, roughly chopped

1 small bunch of thyme

a few parsley stalks (optional)

1 or 2 garlic cloves, bashed

To make the crab stock, bash the crab shells to break them up into pieces and place them with all the other stock ingredients into a large pan with 2 litres (3½ pints) water. Bring to a simmer over a medium–high heat. Cook gently for 1 hour, using a ladle to skim away any froth that rises to the surface. Remove from the heat and cool, then pass through a fine sieve and set aside. You should end up with about 1.2 litres (2 pints) or so of stock.

To make the soup, put the olive oil and butter in a heavy-based pan over a medium heat. When it's bubbling away, add the onion, fennel, carrot, celery, garlic, bay leaf, thyme and tarragon. Cook, stirring regularly, for 4–5 minutes. Add the paprika, fennel seeds and star anise and cook for a further 1 minute, then add the wine and chopped tomatoes. Stir well to combine and cook for a further 4–5 minutes. Add the crab stock, and bring up to gentle simmer. Cook for 25–30 minutes, then remove the soup from the heat and allow it to cool for 20 minutes. Purée the soup in a blender, in batches if necessary, until smooth (you could use a hand blender in the pan, if you prefer – make sure you get a smooth consistency, though).

Pass the soup through a sieve set over a clean pan. You may need to push it through with the back of a spoon or ladle. Return the soup to the heat and bring to a very gentle simmer. Stir in the cream and the brandy, then season with salt and black pepper to taste.

Serve the soup in warmed bowls. You can finish it with a swirl of cream if you like, some cracked black pepper, and a little dressed crab meat – or, as shown here, a cracked crab claw.

Radicchio & crab gratin

Crab is inherently sweet – particularly when it's super-fresh. This is why I've always liked to pair it with something sharp, or in this case a little bitter. Gently frying onions in butter naturally accentuates their sugariness, too (it's worth taking your time here so that you don't let them catch or colour too much). When you finally add the radicchio, you'll balance out all that sweetness. The dash of double cream at the end rounds up the flavours gloriously.

SERVES 2

1 knob of butter

1 small onion, thinly sliced

3 garlic cloves, peeled and thinly sliced

pinch of chilli flakes (optional)

grated zest of ½ lemon

1 smallish red radicchio lettuce (about 150–200g/5½–7oz), shredded

250–300g (9–10½oz) fresh white and brown crab meat

150ml (5fl oz) double cream

salt and freshly ground black pepper

FOR THE GRATIN

100g (3½oz) coarse white breadcrumbs

1 small knob of butter, melted

2 tablespoons grated Parmesan cheese

½ teaspoon chopped rosemary

Melt the butter in a medium heavy-based pan over a medium heat. When it's bubbling add the onions, garlic, chilli (if using) and lemon zest. Season with salt and pepper and cook, stirring regularly, for 8–10 minutes or until the onions are soft and taking on a little colour. Add the radicchio to the pan for 6–8 minutes, until wilted. Then, add the fresh crab meat and the cream, give the whole lot a stir and bring it up to a gentle simmer. Allow the mixture to bubble away for 4–5 minutes, until it thickens slightly, then season with salt and pepper to taste. Transfer the crab and radicchio mixture to an ovenproof dish (about 18–20cm/7–8in diameter).

Heat the oven to 180°C/350°F/gas mark 4. To make the gratin, combine the breadcrumbs with the melted butter, grated Parmesan and chopped rosemary and scatter the mixture over the top of the crab.

Place the dish in the oven and bake for 15–20 minutes until the creamy crab mixture is bubbling and the breadcrumbs are golden. Serve straight away with a green salad.

Oysters with sweet cicely & gooseberries

The herb garden is breathing in deep and begins to breach. There are pockets of white among all the greens. Sweet cicely in full flush has delicate milk-white flowers and vibrant emerald leaves. This herb is sweet by name and by nature, which is why it works beautifully with fresh, sour gooseberries. I like to eat my oysters with something that brings acidity. The gooseberry and sweet-cicely thing does just that, without having to work too hard. It's pretty amazing.

SERVES 2

75g (2½oz) firm gooseberries, topped and tailed

1 tablespoon cider vinegar

2 teaspoons sugar

1 small bunch of sweet cicely leaves, roughly chopped, plus flowers, if available

12 oysters in their shells

salt and freshly ground black pepper

Slice the gooseberries into roughly 5mm (¼in) rounds and place them in a bowl. Add the cider vinegar, sugar, and half the sweet cicely leaves, then season with salt and pepper. Allow the gooseberries to sit in the vinegar mixture while you shuck the oysters (see below).

To shuck an oyster you'll need an oyster knife (one with a sturdy, short blade) and a tea towel to protect your hand from the sharp shell as you grip it. Hold the oyster cupped-side down in the tea towel with the hinge facing towards you. Hold firmly on a chopping board. Insert the knife tip downwards between the two halves of the shell at the pointed back end, where the hinge is located. Once you have the tip of the knife in, you can lever the shell open a little. Slip the knife along the underside of the top half of the shell, which will sever the oyster's adductor muscle, allowing the shell to open fully. Carefully slide the knife blade underneath the oyster to release it completely. Try to save any liquor in the shell.

To serve, place the oysters in their half shells on a suitable serving plate or board. Spoon a little gooseberry mixture onto each oyster, tear over the remaining sweet cicely leaves and serve with a scattering of cicely flowers if you have them.

Smoked oysters with beetroot, horseradish, crème fraîche & dill

This recipe is not difficult, none of it: not cooking the sweet, earthy beetroot, not making the bright dill dressing, not even the quick task of hot-smoking the oysters (you'll need a few small pieces of hard wood for this). It's all simple and fun. The difficult bit is dealing with the fact you've eaten it… you've eaten it and there is none left… .

SERVES 2

6 small beetroot, plus any leaves

1 teaspoon extra-virgin olive oil

2 tablespoons crème fraîche

1 small bunch of dill, chopped

2 teaspoons horseradish sauce

3 or 4 thyme sprigs, plus extra to serve

8 oysters, shucked (see p. 54) and left in their half-shells

2 slices rye bread

butter, for spreading

salt and freshly ground black pepper

Twist the tops off the beetroot, if they have them, and reserve any nice, tender leaves. Give the beetroots a quick wash and place them in a pan along with a good pinch of salt. Cover with water, place the pan over a high heat and bring the water to the boil. Cook for 15–25 minutes, until you can pierce them easily with a knife. (Cooking time will vary depending on how large and how fresh the beetroots are.)

Drain the beetroots and leave them to cool. Once they have cooled, quarter the larger beetroots and halve the smaller ones. Drizzle over the olive oil and season with salt and pepper. Set aside.

In a small bowl combine the crème fraîche with most of the dill and the horseradish. Season with salt and pepper. Stir well to combine.

Place a large heavy-based pan with a close-fitting lid over a high heat. Drop in a small handful of hard-wood pieces (such as oak or beech, or any fruit wood) and the thyme sprigs, then replace the lid. The wood will begin to smoke after a few minutes. Lift the lid and add the oysters so they sit levelly in their shells between the chunks of wood. Replace the lid. Smoke the oysters in the pan for 3–4 minutes, until the oysters have retracted a little, are firm to the touch and cooked through, then lift them out by their shells. (You may have to smoke the oysters in two batches.)

Toast the rye bread, allow to cool slightly, then spread generously with butter. Place one slice of toast on each plate, divide the beetroot equally between them and spoon over the crème fraîche. Remove the warm smoked oysters from their shells and place them on top. Finish each plate with a scattering more of dill, and serve.

Oysters in chicken stock with chives

Come, sit with me and talk about the sea and the land. Tell me how something so clear can be so deep. Break these shells for me and let the flood run. Together, they are somewhere between earth and saltwater. Let's drink the broth and take the oysters with it.

This is one of the most delicious and simple ways I know to enjoy oysters. Think over your chicken stock, pause and taste from time to time. It should be deep-flavoured and clear.

SERVES 2

500ml (17fl oz) well-flavoured chicken stock

6 oysters, shucked (see p. 54), liquor reserved

1 small bunch of chives, chopped, plus any flowers, if available

salt and freshly ground black pepper

FOR THE CHICKEN STOCK (MAKES 1–1.5 LITRES/1¾–2½ PINTS)

2 carcasses of freshly roasted chicken, and any other bits left in the roasting tray

1–2 onions, sliced

2 large carrots, roughly chopped

3–4 celery sticks, roughly chopped

½ a leek, roughly sliced

2–3 garlic cloves, bashed

6 sprigs of thyme

a few parsley stalks

3–4 bay leaves

1 teaspoon black peppercorns

First, make the chicken stock. Tear the carcasses into several pieces and pack them, along with any skin, fat, jelly, bones or other tasty morsels from the roasting tray into a large pan. Add all the vegetables, as well as the herbs and peppercorns, packing them in nice and neatly. Pour over 1.5 litres (2½ pints) of water to cover. Place the pan over a medium heat and bring up to a very low simmer. Reduce the heat to low and simmer gently, uncovered, for 2–3 hours, topping up the water during cooking, if necessary.

Pass the cooked stock through a very fine sieve into a clean bowl or container, allow to cool, then cover and refrigerate.

To make the dish, remove any fat from the surface of the chilled stock. Pour 500ml (17fl oz) of the stock into a medium pan and set over a medium–high heat. Bring the stock to a simmer, taste and season with salt and pepper. (Seasoning the stock will bring out all its flavour.)

Warm two large soup plates. When you're ready to serve, put 3 oysters into the bottom of each plate. Pour the oyster liquor into the chicken stock. Stir, then bring the stock back up to simmering point.

Remove the stock from the heat and immediately pour it over the oysters to lightly poach them in the plate. Scatter over the chives, and any flowers, if available. Season with salt and pepper, then serve straight away.

Crispy gut weed with potato cakes

Gut weed is the sort of seaweed that cloaks exposed rocks in robes of green and then, as the tide floods it rises to the water — a thousand thread-like forms, swaying in the back-and-forth of the waves. This recipe shows you how to prepare this wonderful wild food — it tastes brilliant when fried until crisp.

SERVES 2

1 good handful of gut weed, washed in several changes of water until clean

450g (1lb) floury potatoes, such as Maris Piper or King Edward, peeled and cut into 3–4cm (1¼–1½in) cubes

2 teaspoons salt, plus extra for seasoning

1 knob of butter

2 shallots or 1 small onion, finely sliced

1 or 2 thyme sprigs, leaves picked

30g (1oz) Cheddar cheese, grated

sunflower oil, for deep frying

3 tablespoons extra-virgin olive oil

freshly ground black pepper

Prepare the gut weed well in advance. Squeeze out all the excess water from washing, then layer it out over a clean, dry tea towel set over a tray. Let it dry for several hours in the sun (outside or on a sunny windowsill) or in the fridge.

When the gut weed is dry, place the potato pieces in a large pan and cover them with plenty of fresh water. Add the salt and bring the water to the boil. Boil the potatoes for 20–30 minutes, or until they are nice and tender. Then, drain them in a colander and leave them there for 15 minutes to allow the steam to evaporate.

Meanwhile, place a medium frying pan over a low heat. Add half the butter, then the sliced shallots or onion. Add the thyme leaves, stir, and season. Cook, stirring regularly, until the onions are soft and just beginning to colour (about 15–20 minutes).

Tip the potatoes into a bowl and mash them really well. Fold through the cooked shallot or onion, the remaining butter, and the Cheddar, and season well. Form the potato mixture into 2 generous cakes and chill, covered, in the fridge for at least 1 hour.

To cook the gut weed, fill a large pan 7–10cm (3–4in) deep with sunflower oil and bring the oil to a heat of 160°C/320°F (or until a cube of bread dropped into the oil fizzes and turns golden). Cook the gut weed in small batches for 30–60 seconds, until it's stopped fizzing but is still emerald green. Remove each batch with a slotted spoon and drain on kitchen paper. Scatter with salt and set aside.

Heat the olive oil in a medium non-stick frying pan over a medium heat. When hot, add the potato cakes and fry for 4–5 minutes on each side, until crisp and golden. Serve the potato cakes straight away with the crispy seaweed over the top, or on the side. (This is also lovely with a fried egg on top of the potato cake.)

Beef shin with smoked dulse

With its striking oxblood hue, transparent when held up to the light, dulse seaweed is easy to recognize. It washes up on the beach, ready for gathering, often along the high-tide line, and looks like massive splayed hands and fingers. I collect it, wash it and cold smoke it for 8 to 12 hours to impart a flavour that is quite incredible. Dulse adds waves of intensity to this slowly cooked shin of beef, but you don't have to smoke your own weed (so to speak) — you can buy ready-smoked dulse from companies that specialize in foraged seaweeds (try maraseaweed.com and irishseaweeds.com).

SERVES 4

2 tablespoons extra-virgin olive oil or beef dripping

About 800g (1lb 12oz) shin of beef, in thick slices on or off the bone

2 onions, sliced

4 large garlic cloves, peeled and thinly sliced

2 celery sticks, trimmed and thinly sliced

3 or 4 thyme sprigs

½ glass of red wine

2–3 teaspoons powdered smoked dulse, or 1 handful home-smoked dulse

300ml (10½fl oz) chicken stock (see p. 58) or water

salt and freshly ground black pepper

Heat the oven to 120°C/235°F/gas mark 1.

Heat the oil or dripping in a large heavy-based flameproof casserole. Season the pieces of shin with salt and pepper, then put them in the pan to brown for 3–4 minutes on each side, until well-coloured all over. Remove from the pan and set aside on a plate.

Add the onions, garlic, celery and thyme to the pan and cook gently over a low heat, stirring regularly until the onions are soft but not coloured. Return the meat to the pan, then add the wine, dulse and stock or water and bring to a gentle simmer.

Place a lid on the casserole and put it in the oven for 4–5 hours, or until the meat shreds easily with a fork. Remove the casserole from the oven, season to taste, and allow the meat to rest for 25 minutes before serving with buttery mash.

Laver bread with oats, clams & ham

John Wright, an experienced forager and good friend, first introduced me to laver – a seaweed that is smooth in texture and unimaginably slender, being only one cell thick. It also has a reluctance to tenderize to the point of frustration! (But, once it's cooked it's wonderful.) Purple laver is one of the most common of several similar species, often found clinging to rocks. It has an amazing iodine flavour that works beautifully with the sweet clams and crisp salty ham in this recipe.

SERVES 4

1 bowl of laver seaweed, trimmed and washed thoroughly, or 1 jar of pre-cooked laver

4 large slices of prosciutto

25g (1oz) porridge oats

1 knob of butter

1 garlic clove, peeled and grated

750g (1lb 10oz) clams in their shells, washed

4 slices white sourdough, granary or rye bread

salt and freshly ground black pepper

Heat the oven to 120°C/235°F/gas mark 1. If you're using fresh laver, first wash it in several changes of water so that it is completely grit-free. To cook, roughly chop the laver, place it in a large heavy-based pan and cover with fresh water. Place a lid on the pan and bring the water up to a simmer. Cook gently for 5–6 hours, or until the laver is tender and the liquid has reduced. If at any point the pan appears dry, add a little more water, until you have a thick, somewhat sticky seaweed. Set the cooked laver aside.

Place the slices of prosciutto onto a parchment-lined baking tray and scatter the oats around. Place in the oven for 12–15 minutes to crisp up the prosciutto and toast the oats.

Place a medium pan on a medium heat. When the pan is hot, add the butter, then the garlic. Cook for 15–20 seconds, until the garlic is soft but not coloured. Tip in the clams along with 2 tablespoons of water, stir, then place a lid on the pan. Cook for 3–4 minutes, shaking the pan regularly to encourage the clams to open. When all the clams are open, use a slotted spoon to lift them out of the pan and set aside, leaving the pan on the heat.

Chop 150–200g (5½–7oz) of the cooked laver and add it to the clam cooking liquor in the pan. Stir well, then season with salt and pepper to taste and cook gently for 5–10 minutes, until the seaweed starts to thicken but is still moist.

Toast the bread on both sides. Top each piece of toast with an equal amount of warm laver, pick the warm clams from their shells and scatter over, then break over shards of the crispy ham. Sprinkle over a few oats and serve straight away.

Sea kale & sea bass

Sea kale is a striking and hardy plant that seems to flourish on bleak, inhospitable pebble beaches. Quite often it will be alone, the only copper-green bloom of life bound and rooted expressively to the hard stones. In spring it buds, producing the most delicious broccoli-like spears. The new leaf growth is so tender you can eat it raw, while the slightly larger leaves respond well to blanching or steaming lightly and serving with butter and good olive oil. Both raw and cooked, the leaves have a gentle salinity, as many of our coastal greens do. In late spring and early summer, the plant blooms, producing dainty, edible white flowers. In the autumn it fruits, producing hundreds of pearl-like berries. In the winter, you can find the dead frames of sea kale plants tumbling about the beach in the wind, often with their berries still attached.

SERVES 6 AS A CANAPÉ

100g (3½oz) impeccably fresh bass fillet, skinned

juice of ½ lemon

1 tablespoon extra-virgin olive oil

12 small sea kale or young curly kale leaves

sea kale flowers, if available

salt and freshly ground black pepper

Place the sea-bass fillet on a board and cut it into thin slices, each no more than 5mm (¼in) thick, across the grain.

Place the fish slices in a small bowl, then add the lemon juice and olive oil and season well with salt and pepper.

Gently wash the sea kale leaves and arrange them on a serving plate or a board. Spoon a little sea bass onto each leaf along with the oil and lemon from the bowl. Serve scattered with kale flowers, if available.

Creamed sea beet & lamb's kidneys

I drive to one particular beach to collect sea beet. It does well there, growing where the weedy gravel car park meets a lengthy strip of waste ground, behind a few knackered dinghies that rattle on their rusty trollies all winter. Like the spikes of an emerald crown, its leaves are thick, green and arrow-shaped. They taste like the finest spinach you've ever had, and are best when young. Creamed sea beet is the ultimate, in so many ways. This one, with seared fresh, tender and subtle lamb's kidneys, is way up there.

SERVES 2

200ml (7fl oz) milk

½ onion, thinly sliced

1 bay leaf

2 thyme sprigs

300–400g (10½–14oz) sea beet, or spinach or chard, coarser stalks removed

1 knob of unsalted butter

15g (½oz) plain flour

4 lamb's kidneys

1 tablespoon extra-virgin olive oil

2 rosemary sprigs

salt and freshly ground black pepper

Pour the milk into a medium pan and place it over a high heat. Add the onion, bay leaf and thyme and bring the mixture to a gentle simmer. Remove the pan from the heat and allow the flavours to infuse the milk for 15–20 minutes.

Meanwhile, bring a large pan of water to the boil. Drop in the prepared sea beet or spinach or chard and cook for 3–4 minutes, until the leaves are tender. Drain the sea beet and refresh by running it under cold water. When the sea beet is cool, squeeze out any liquid, roughly chop, and set aside.

Now make a white sauce. Set a medium pan over a medium heat, add the butter and when bubbling add the flour. Stir and cook for 1 minute, then pour in the infused milk, straining it through a sieve as you do so. Discard the onion and herbs. Use a whisk to work the white sauce as you cook it for 1–2 minutes, until it thickens. Season well with salt and pepper, then turn off the heat and fold in the chopped, cooked sea beet. Cover and keep warm.

Carefully halve the kidneys laterally (across their face). Using the tip of your knife, remove the tough, white core and discard it. Place a medium frying pan over a high heat and add the oil. When it's hot, add the kidney halves and rosemary, and season with salt and pepper. After 1 minute, turn the kidneys and cook for a further 1 minute on the second side. (Don't be tempted to turn them too soon – they should take on some colour.) Turn off the heat and let the kidneys rest in the pan for 4–5 minutes. Serve the kidneys on warm plates alongside the sea beet, and some toast, if you like.

Samphire & prawns with butter & mace

A popular wild sea green, samphire comes from the same family as sea beet (see p. 69). You can find it on tidal mud flats, inlets and estuaries, although always take care not to uproot the plant – or to become rooted in the mud yourself! And if time and tide aren't on your side, this tiny twig of a sea vegetable is also readily available in supermarkets these days. Its fleshy, moist and brackish qualities make samphire a gift for fish; and its peculiar, gnarled form makes it a gift for chefs, too. It's got class, longevity, and an elegance I really like. When I make this dish at home, I tend to use shrimps and I eat them whole, shell and all. I do this because I can, and because it's interesting. But, if you use larger prawns you might find the 'whole shell-on approach' texturally challenging...

SERVES 4

250g (9oz) marsh samphire, coarser stems trimmed

1 knob of butter

2 tablespoons extra-virgin olive oil

2 garlic cloves, peeled and very thinly sliced

½ teaspoon chilli flakes

zest of ½ lemon and the juice of 1 whole lemon

½ teaspoon ground mace

400g (14oz) shell-on cooked prawns or shrimps or live prawns or shrimps

salt and freshly ground black pepper

Bring a medium pan of water to the boil. Drop in the samphire and cook for 3–4 minutes, until tender. Drain and set aside.

Heat the butter and olive oil in a large frying pan over a medium heat. When bubbling, add the garlic, chilli flakes, lemon zest and mace. Cook, stirring regularly, for 1–2 minutes, until the garlic is just beginning to colour around the edges. Add the drained samphire to the pan and toss well.

If you have live prawns or shrimps, blanch them in salted boiling water for a few minutes until they've lost their translucency and are cooked through.

Scatter over the cooked shellfish, add the lemon juice, season well with salt and pepper, and remove from the heat as soon as the prawns or shrimps are warm. Divide the mixture equally onto four plates and serve straight away with good bread and butter.

Pickled mussels with radishes, toasted coriander & apples

There is something of Normandy in this fresh salad: a bicycle ride down the Route du Cidre; a peppery-pink radish with delightfully fresh, cold butter; a bowl of plump, yellow wild mussels, cooked in cream on some beach off Gouville-sur-Mer. It's almost like you taste it in French. This dish is about perfectly cooked mussels, sweet, crunchy apple, and the acidity of good cider vinegar – and how they all play out when they get together. I love the orangey air that toasted coriander seed brings to the delicate pickle – it's well worth a try. You can prepare the mussels the day before, but I like them best once they have cooled and before they see the fridge.

SERVES 2

2 bay leaves

2 thyme sprigs

500g (1lb 2oz) mussels, cleaned

1 tablespoon good-quality cider vinegar

½ teaspoon golden caster sugar

2 teaspoons small coriander seeds, toasted

1 dessert apple

4–6 firm radishes, with tops, if available

salt and freshly ground black pepper

Place a large pan over a high heat. Add 100ml (3½fl oz) water, the bay leaves and thyme sprigs. When the water is boiling hard, tip in the mussels and place a close-fitting lid on the pan. Cook, shaking the pan once or twice, for 1–2 minutes, or until the mussel shells are all just open. Turn off the heat, then drain the mussels into a colander set over a bowl to catch the cooking liquor. Discard any mussels that haven't opened up.

When the mussels are cool enough to handle, remove the meat from the shells and place it in a bowl, reserving the drained cooking liquor. Add the cider vinegar, sugar, coriander seeds and 2 tablespoons of the cooking liquor to the mussel meat, stir through, then season with a little salt and pepper.

To serve, quarter and core the apple and then cut each quarter into 2 or 3 wedges. Divide the apple pieces roughly between two plates. Slice the radish into 2–3mm ($\frac{1}{16}$–$\frac{1}{8}$in) rounds and scatter them over the apple, along with any radish top leaves, if available. Finally, spoon over the mussels along with plenty of their coriander-spiked dressing, and serve immediately.

Mussels with watercress, watercress purée & bacon

Here are the three things I was thinking about when I invented this dish. First, my favourite soup of all might be watercress, if it were made as I like it: brilliant green, rich and seasoned to the hilt. Second, like many others, I'm massively partial to the salty sweetness of good, crisp streaky bacon. Third, I have a healthy love for freshly cooked mussels, in all their guises. So, this dish is the child of those ideas, those culinary 'wants'. Conceived and delivered at my kitchen table, its creation was a quiet labour during a morning well spent. As soon as the mussels are cooked, wilt the watercress and make the purée: move fast and serve everything nice and hot.

SERVES 2 AS A LIGHT SUPPER OR A LUNCH

extra-virgin olive oil, for frying

2–4 rashers smoked or unsmoked streaky bacon

1 small knob of butter

½ small onion, sliced

1 garlic clove, peeled and sliced

1kg (2lb 4oz) mussels, cleaned

150g (5½oz) watercress, plus extra for serving

salt and freshly ground black pepper

Place a medium frying pan over a medium–high heat. Add a dash of oil followed by the bacon. Cook the bacon for 6–8 minutes, until golden and crisp, or to your liking. Keep warm.

Heat a large pan over a medium heat. Add the butter and a spoonful of bacon fat from the frying pan. When the fat mixture is bubbling, add the onion and garlic, and season with a little salt and pepper. Cook the onion and garlic for 2–3 minutes, until the onion is soft but not coloured, then add the mussels along with 2 tablespoons of water. Place a lid on the pan and give it a gentle shake. Cook the mussels for 1–2 minutes, or until the mussel shells are all just open. Discard any mussels that haven't opened up.

Using a slotted spoon, remove the mussels from the pan to a warm, large bowl, leaving the pan (with the onion and cooking liquor) on the heat. Cover the mussels with a clean tea towel and keep as warm as possible. Throw the watercress into the pan and cook for 1–2 minutes until wilted, then tip the contents of the pan straight into a food processor and purée until smooth.

Place a generous spoonful of purée onto each plate. Divide the mussels equally between the two plates, and finish with a piece of crisp bacon and a little fresh watercress. Serve straight away.

Mussels with lovage, celery & cream

I'm particularly taken by lovage before I even taste it – it just *sounds* good; 'lovage' sounds like the place of a love-in where everyone and everything is gorgeous. You might not think it on first taste, but this easy-to-grow plant, although heavily scented, is a versatile herb. I use it a few times in this book: with rhubarb and goat's cheese (see p. 18), with sweet roast beetroot and wet garlic (p. 94) – and here, with handsome mussels and earthy celery, all indulgently augmented by double cream. It wouldn't be a love-in without double cream.

SERVES 3–4

1 knob of butter

1 tablespoon extra-virgin olive oil

3 celery sticks, sliced into 4–5mm (⅛–¼in) pieces

1 onion, halved and very thinly sliced

4 thyme sprigs

2 or 3 garlic cloves, peeled and sliced

4 or 5 lovage leaves, roughly chopped

3–4 tablespoons double cream

1kg (2lb 4oz) mussels, cleaned

salt and freshly ground black pepper

Heat the butter and olive oil in a large, heavy-based pan over a medium heat. When they're bubbling, add the sliced celery. Cook the celery, stirring regularly, for 4–5 minutes, or until it starts to soften slightly. Add the onion, thyme and garlic, lightly season with salt and pepper, and stir well. Cook for a further 3–4 minutes, until the onion is soft but not coloured. Now turn up the heat to high and add the lovage and cream. As soon as the cream begins to boil, throw in the mussels. Stir carefully, then immediately place a tight-fitting lid on the pan. Cook for 2–4 minutes, giving the pan a good shake every so often, until the mussel shells are all just open. Remove the pan from the heat and discard any mussels that haven't opened up.

You can serve the mussels in individual bowls or leave them in the cooking pot, or transfer them to a large, shallow dish, and bring them to the table that way.

garden

garden

Bumble bees, warm mornings, dew from the night, clear and beautifully bright. Memories, wheelbarrow rides, me inside. The climbing frame, beans, peas and the scythe. An unnetted fruit cage, birdsong, high sun, parsley, rosemary and sage. We eat, your eyes are full of pride. The air in the shed is cool and of earth, stone and metal. Tomatoes become ripe, the gardener moves from row to row. Baskets of flowers and salad. Potato plants lie drying on the heap. Nothing is asleep.

courgettes

tomatoes

beetroot

lettuce

gooseberries

Raw courgettes with fennel, pea, mint, dill & lemon

It's worth picking up a little courgette plant from your local garden centre just so you can make this salad, even just once or twice, with the freshest, finest courgettes. A plant pot outside your back door may be all you need. If you can't grow your own, though, seek out really fresh little courgettes; they should be no bigger than your middle finger and as firm as wood in the hand. Their nutty flavour takes this beautifully clean salad to another level. Crisp fennel bulb with its muted aniseed, and raw peas in the pod, freed straight into the bowl, create lovely textures that bound around in lemon and dill and mint – the perfect salad-bowl bedfellows.

SERVES 2

250g (9oz) very fresh peas in the pod or about 100g (3½oz) frozen peas

4–6 small, very fresh courgettes

1 fennel bulb, trimmed

juice and zest of 1 lemon

3 tablespoons extra-virgin olive oil

3 or 4 mint sprigs, leaves picked and thinly ribboned, a few left whole

1 small bunch of dill, fronds picked from the stem

salt and freshly ground black pepper

Pod the peas if you're using fresh, and set aside. If not, bring a small pan of salted water to the boil and add the frozen peas. Cook the frozen peas for 1–2 minutes, until they are just tender, then drain them in a colander and refresh them by running them under cold water. Drain again and set aside.

Trim the courgettes, then slice them thinly into rounds of about 2mm (1⁄16in) thick. Very finely slice the fennel bulb down its face, from top to bottom. Make sure your slices are as thin as you can get them. (You can use a mandoline for this, but ensure you use the cutting guard.)

Place the sliced courgettes, sliced fennel and cooked peas in a bowl and add the lemon juice and zest, and the olive oil, mint ribbons and leaves and dill fronds, and generously season with salt and pepper. Use your hands to tumble everything together gently and bring to the table.

Barbecued courgettes with quail eggs & tartare sauce

Charred courgette is just so good. Aim to scorch and blister: if the barbecue's white hot, the courgettes will char in minutes but retain a little bite. Alternatively, you can cook them as I have here, over a slightly lower heat, for a little longer, so they soften but blacken in places, too.

SERVES 4

8–12 quail eggs

6–8 small–medium-sized, firm courgettes

4 tablespoons extra-virgin olive oil

juice and zest of ½ lemon

1 small bunch of mixed flat-leaf parsley leaves and fennel fronds

salt and black pepper

FOR THE TARTARE SAUCE

2 large egg yolks

1 teaspoon English mustard

2 teaspoons cider vinegar

1 anchovy fillet

pinch of sugar

1 small garlic clove, peeled and grated

200ml (7fl oz) sunflower oil

3 tablespoons extra-virgin olive oil

8–10 small gherkins

2–3 teaspoons capers

1 spring onion, finely chopped

1 tablespoon chopped dill

1 tablespoon chopped parsley

1 hard-boiled egg, chopped

lemon juice, to taste

salt and black pepper

To make the tartare sauce, place the yolks in a food processor with the mustard, vinegar, anchovy, sugar and garlic. Season, then blitz for 30–40 seconds to combine. Mix the oils in a jug, then with the processor running, trickle the oil mixture into the egg mixture, a few drops at a time to start with, then in a steady stream until you've used up the oil and you have a thick mayonnaise. If it's too thick, stir in 1–2 tablespoons of warm water. Roughly chop the gherkins and capers, and fold them into the mayo with the spring onion, herbs and chopped egg. Season and adjust the acidity with a dash of lemon, if required.

To make the dish, bring a medium pan of water to the boil. Add the quail eggs and cook for 2½–3 minutes, then use a slotted spoon to transfer the eggs to a bowl of iced water. Once the eggs have cooled, gently roll each one on a work surface to crack the shell slightly, then place it back into the iced water (to make the shell easier to remove). Shell the eggs one by one and set aside.

Top and tail the courgettes and slice them lengthways into strips about 3mm (⅛in) thick. Place into a large bowl and season with some salt and pepper. Add 2 tablespoons of olive oil and the lemon zest and tumble together.

Light your barbecue. When the embers are glowing and hot, lay your courgettes on the grill and cook for 8–12 minutes on each side, or until you have an even, light charring with some caramelization. (Alternatively, lay them over a very hot chargrill pan and cook for 2–3 minutes on each side.) Remove from the heat and arrange the courgettes on a platter. Halve the quail eggs and place them in and around the courgettes. Generously spoon over the tartare sauce, drizzle over the lemon juice, trickle with the remaining olive oil and sprinkle with the parsley and the fennel fronds. Serve warm with fresh bread.

Courgette flowers with salt cod

This generous recipe gives and gives until it's gone. I like courgette flowers with the young courgettes still attached – it adds an extra texture when you come to eat them... with your fingers, your friends and some chilled fino.

SERVES 6

250g (9oz) pollack or cod fillet

150g (5½oz) fine sea salt, plus extra for seasoning

200g (7oz) floury potatoes, such as King Edward or Maris Piper, peeled and cut into 3–4cm (1¼–1½in) cubes

6 tablespoons extra-virgin olive oil

2–3 large garlic cloves, peeled and finely chopped

2 tablespoons double cream

12–14 small courgettes with large flowers, or 12–14 courgette flowers

1 tablespoon pumpkin seeds, toasted

freshly ground black pepper

good pinch of smoked paprika, to serve

FOR THE BATTER

50g (1¾oz) plain flour

50g (1¾oz) cornflour

good pinch of salt

sunflower oil, for deep frying

Place the fish in a bowl and scatter over the salt. Turn to coat, then cover and refrigerate for 5–6 hours. Wash the salt off the fish under a cold tap. Place the fish in a pan, cover with water and bring to a simmer over a medium heat. Cook for 4–5 minutes, or until the fish is just cooked through. Remove the fish from the pan and allow to cool. Pick over the fish, discarding any skin and bones, then flake the flesh. Put the potatoes in a pan with plenty of water. Bring to the boil and cook for 15–20 minutes, until tender. Drain and mash.

Heat 5 tablespoons of olive oil in a small pan over a low heat. Add the garlic and sweat for a few minutes, until it just starts to colour at the edges. Remove and tip into a food processor along with the fish flakes. Pulse until you have a fairly smooth consistency. Tip the fish mixture out into a mixing bowl and beat in the mashed potato and the cream. Season with black pepper (it won't need salt).

Hold the base of one courgette flower and gently fold down the petals over your index finger and thumb. Using a teaspoon, spoon some of the salt-cod mixture into the flower, then press down to remove any air pockets. Fold the petals back into place. Repeat with the remaining flowers. In a small bowl, combine the pumpkin seeds with the remaining olive oil, and season well. To make the batter, combine the flour, cornflour and salt, then whisk in about 150ml (5fl oz) water until well-combined.

Place a large saucepan on a high heat and add the frying oil to come 5cm (2in) up the sides of the pan. When frying-hot (see p. 211), turn the stuffed courgette flowers in the batter and, 2–4 flowers at a time, lower them quickly into the hot oil. Don't overcrowd the pan. Fry for about 2 minutes, until lightly golden and crisp, then drain on kitchen paper. Repeat as necessary. To serve, place 2 or 3 flowers on a plate. Scatter over the pumpkin seeds and finish with a sprinkling of smoked paprika.

Roast tomatoes on toast with tarragon & thyme

I like the idea that something could become bigger, bolder, fuller and more intense as it withers, contracts, softens and breaks — it seems a great irony. This is exactly what happens when you slowly cook sweet, ripe tomatoes in a warm oven. They intensify, exaggerating everything that's already there: colour, sugar, complexity. The heat caramelizes them, but also brings a trace of bitterness. Tarragon, with its intense, aniseed flavour, is the most amazing herb to use with tomatoes, so I don't hold back — it gently perfumes the tomatoes during cooking.

SERVES 4

About 700g (1lb 9oz) ripe, heritage tomatoes — mixed sizes, colours and shapes

16 garlic cloves, peeled

1 bunch of tarragon

4 or 5 thyme sprigs

3–4 tablespoons extra-virgin olive oil

4 slices rustic bread, or sourdough

salt and freshly ground black pepper

Heat the oven to 140–150°C/275–300°F/gas mark 1–2.

To prepare your tomatoes, cut any larger ones into quarters or eighths and a handful of the smaller tomatoes in half. Place these on a baking tray, cut side up. Leave the rest of the tomatoes whole and scatter them onto the baking tray, too. Tuck the whole garlic cloves between the tomatoes.

Prepare the herbs by leaving any tender stems whole, and picking the leaves of any tougher ones. Discard the tough stems and then scatter the tender stems and picked leaves over the tomatoes. Drizzle over the olive oil and season well with salt and pepper.

Place the baking tray in the oven and roast for 1½–2 hours, until the tomatoes are collapsed and caramelized. When the tomatoes are ready, remove them from the oven and allow them to cool for a few minutes while you toast the bread.

Spoon the soft tomatoes on to the toast, along with a few garlic cloves, any roasting juices and lots of the crispy herbs, and serve straight away.

Fish soup with tomatoes & star anise

I've been making variations of this soup for ages. Here, I use pollack, squid and mussels, but clams would be great instead of mussels, and some crab meat would be incredible. You can swap the pollack for any sustainable white fish: pouting, gurnard and grey mullet are all perfect.

SERVES 6–8

5 tablespoons extra-virgin olive oil

1 large fennel bulb, finely chopped

2 garlic cloves, peeled and thinly sliced

2 onions, finely chopped

3 celery sticks, finely chopped

2 teaspoons fennel seeds

2 teaspoons paprika

1 star anise

1 small red chilli, deseeded and thinly sliced (optional)

pinch of saffron

1 glass of white wine

600g (1lb 5oz) ripe tomatoes, peeled, deseeded and chopped, or 1 x 400g (14oz) tin chopped tomatoes

750ml (26fl oz) fish stock or water

750g (1lb 10oz) pollack fillets

2 small squid, sliced into rounds

300g (10½oz) mussels, cleaned

1 squeeze of lemon juice

fennel fronds and flat-leaf parsley leaves, for sprinkling

salt and black pepper

Heat 1 tablespoon of the olive oil in a large saucepan or casserole over a medium–low heat. Add the chopped fennel, and the garlic, onion and celery and cook gently, stirring often, for 12–15 minutes, until the onion is nice and soft. Add the fennel seeds, paprika, star anise, chilli (if using) and saffron, stir again, and cook for a further 5 minutes. Add the white wine, bring to the boil over a high heat, then add in the chopped tomatoes and their juice, and bring back to a simmer. Reduce the heat and cook gently, stirring occasionally for about 30 minutes, then pour in the fish stock or water. Simmer for a further 20 minutes.

Meanwhile prepare the fish. Place the fillets on a board and use a sharp knife to cut the fish flesh away from the skin. Cut the flesh into large pieces of about 3–4cm (1¼–1½in) each. Place the pieces in a bowl with the squid rounds and season with salt and pepper.

Drop the mussels into the simmering soup. Cover the pan and cook for 2–3 minutes. Uncover, give the pan a swirl, then add the fish and squid and turn them gently through the sauce. Cover again and cook for another 3–4 minutes, or until the fish is just cooked and all the mussels are open. Discard any mussels that haven't opened up.

Taste the soup and adjust the seasoning as required. Stir in the remaining extra-virgin olive oil and a squeeze of lemon juice, then serve in bowls with a sprinkling of fennel fronds and parsley, and hunks of good-quality bread on the side.

Fresh tomato salad

I wanted to include a raw tomato recipe that was totally unpretentious and really easy. This is one of those salads I want to eat every time the sun is hot and the wine is cold. I need it when the bread is fresh with a splintered and cracked floury crust, the basil scent is strong, and the olive oil is peppery and deep green. Everything that was good, or ever will be good about thinly sliced red onion is showcased here. It is a song to the sun and to a fruit that, when allowed to ripen outside, in the sun, is one of the most delicious things you can eat.

SERVES 4

1kg (2lb 4oz) ripe tomatoes of different sizes and colours

½ red onion, halved and very thinly sliced

1 large handful of basil, large leaves picked, smaller leaves on tender stems

3 tablespoons extra-virgin olive oil

4 tablespoons red wine vinegar

1 teaspoon golden caster sugar

salt and freshly ground black pepper

First, prepare your tomatoes. Using a very sharp knife (serrated can be good), cut the tomatoes from top to bottom into 1cm (½in) slices. Season all the tomato slices lightly with salt and black pepper, then arrange them onto a large serving platter, starting with the larger tomato slices at the bottom and layering up so that the smaller ones are on the top. Scatter the onion slices over the tomatoes, followed by all the basil leaves.

Make a dressing by combining the oil, red wine vinegar and sugar in a small jug and whisking until the sugar dissolves. Season the dressing with salt and pepper, and stir again. Drizzle the dressing all over the tomatoes and onions, then allow the salad to rest for 5−10 minutes before serving.

Roast beetroot & wet garlic with bay, lovage & thyme

I remember sitting down to eat this with a friend, casually, and with no big expectation. It was just another lovely-sounding combination I wanted to have a go at cooking. Partway through eating, we both slowed, then stopped. There was an easy silence. Both he and I wore a face of joy, coloured by the flush of mild wonder. It was one of those rare lunches that was delicious on every level: crushed, sweet roasted garlic, squeezed like purée from its papery skin; dark claret beetroot giving pure earth and sugar; and lovage, a tumbling wave breaking over everything.

SERVES 2

4 or 5 beetroots of mixed colours, trimmed and scrubbed

5 or 6 wet garlic heads

1 bunch of thyme sprigs

8–10 bay leaves, torn

1 small bunch of lovage, leaves picked and torn

2–3 tablespoons extra-virgin olive oil

salt and freshly ground black pepper

Heat the oven to 180°C/350°F/gas mark 4. Place the beetroots in a large pan and cover with water. Place the pan over a high heat, bring the water up to a simmer and cook the beetroots, uncovered, for 20–25 minutes, until they yield to the point of a knife.

When the beetroots are ready, drain them and leave them to cool in the colander. When they're cool enough to handle, slip off the skins and place the beetroots in a roasting tray. If they're big, halve or quarter them so that all the pieces are roughly the same size. Add the whole garlic heads, the thyme (on the stalks), and the torn bay and lovage leaves. Season with salt and pepper and drizzle all over with the olive oil.

Place the roasting tray in the oven and bake for 35–45 minutes, until the garlic is soft and tender and the beetroots are beginning to crisp and blister.

Place 2 or 3 of the roasted garlic bulbs on a plate, with a spoonful of beetroot and herbs alongside. This is excellent served with toasted sourdough.

Grilled sardines with beetroot, cumin & rosemary

The last time I made this summery roast, I also made a big pile of flat breads. They were so good, being a little blistered, crisp and soft all at the same the time. We piled the cumin-spiked beetroot onto the flat breads and then lifted the tender fillets from the grilled sardines and laid them over the top. We spooned over the cool minted yoghurt and rolled it all up into the most ridiculously good sardine-and-beetroot wraps. It was a top way to eat this full-flavoured yet underrated oily fish — but it's just as good more conventionally, alongside a good, simply dressed green salad.

SERVES 3–4

1kg (2lb 4oz) small beetroots of mixed colours, trimmed and scrubbed

3 tablespoons extra-virgin olive oil

3 or 4 rosemary sprigs

8–12 fresh sardines, gutted and scaled

2 large garlic cloves, peeled and grated

2–3 teaspoons cumin seeds, lightly crushed

1 small bunch of mint, leaves picked and chopped

2–3 tablespoons plain natural yoghurt

salt and freshly ground black pepper

Heat the oven to 200°C/400°F/gas mark 6. Place the beetroots in a large pan and cover with water. Place the pan over a high heat, bring the water up to a simmer and cook the beetroots, uncovered, for 20–25 minutes, until they yield to the point of a knife.

When the beetroots are ready, drain them and leave them to cool in the colander. When they're cool enough to handle, slip off the skins and place the beetroots in a roasting tray. If they're big, halve or quarter them so that all the beetroot pieces are roughly the same size. Drizzle over 2 tablespoons of the olive oil, scatter over the rosemary sprigs and season with salt and pepper.

Place the roasting tray in the oven and cook the beetroot pieces for 20–30 minutes, until golden and blistered in places. Remove the tray from the oven and lay the sardines among the beetroot. Turn off the oven and heat the grill to high.

In a small bowl, combine the garlic and the crushed cumin seeds with the remaining olive oil. Brush or spoon the garlicky, cumin-infused oil over the fish and season everything well with salt and pepper. Place the roasting tray under the grill and cook everything for 6–8 minutes, or until the sardines are golden and their skin is starting to crisp. Meanwhile, in a small bowl mix the mint into the natural yoghurt, stirring to combine thoroughly. When the sardines are ready, bring the roasting tray to the table and serve everything with the minty yoghurt alongside.

A salad of raw beetroot, curd & rose

It's difficult not to be taken in by the look of this fresh, raw salad with its calm class and subtle beauty. However, what's really lovely is how it tastes. Its sweetness comes from very thinly sliced fresh raw beetroots (the fresher you can get them, the sweeter they'll be); its fragrance comes from the punch of toasted cracked coriander seeds and orange zest, and the gentle flavour of rosewater and edible rose petals. For its creamy richness, I love using ewe's curd, but a fresh, soft goat's cheese or even a good mascarpone would be fine.

SERVES 4 AS A STARTER

5 or 6 beetroots of mixed colours and all roughly golf-ball sized

juice and zest of 1 orange

1–2 teaspoons rosewater

2 tablespoons extra-virgin olive oil

150g (5½oz) ewe's curd, or soft goat's cheese, or mascarpone

2 teaspoons small coriander seeds, toasted, then crushed

a scattering of dried, edible rose petals (optional)

salt and freshly ground black pepper

Scrub or peel the beetroots depending on the thickness of the skin – if the beetroots are very fresh, you might be able just to give them a good-old scrub. Use a mandoline or a very sharp knife to slice the beetroots into about 1mm (1⁄32in) rounds (certainly no thicker than 2mm/1⁄16in), and place the rounds in a bowl.

In a separate bowl make the dressing by combining the orange juice and zest with the rosewater and olive oil, then finish off with a pinch of salt and a twist of black pepper. Spoon half the dressing over the beetroot rounds, tumble together using your hands, and allow the salad to rest for 15–20 minutes to soften the beetroot and allow the flavours to marry, mingle and mellow for a while.

To serve, dot large spoonfuls of ewe's curd (or goat's cheese or mascarpone) over a serving platter (or spread it in a layer, if you prefer). Scatter over the dressed beetroot, sprinkle over the coriander seeds and the rose petals, if using, and drizzle over a little more dressing before bringing to the table.

Lettuce with black pudding, thyme croûtons, & mustard dressing

A good butterhead is a really unique lettuce – it's tender, bright, light and incredibly quenching to eat. I like it most sodden in mustardy French dressing (as here), and I even like it when it goes soft, like it's been dressed for supper, uneaten and left out all night. However, it's not just the dressed leaves of the butterhead that make this warm salad so good. Proper, sweet black pudding, fried crisp on the outside and fatty-soft in the middle, and crunchy croûtons untempered in the folds of the leaves make the whole thing magical.

SERVES 2

1 small or ½ large butterhead lettuce

200g (7oz) good-quality black pudding (see p. 31)

1 tablespoon light oil or olive oil, for frying

4 slices rustic white bread, or sourdough

1 knob of butter, for frying

1 small bunch of thyme sprigs, leaves picked

2 large or 4 small spring onions, trimmed and sliced

salt and freshly ground black pepper

FOR THE DRESSING

2 teaspoons Dijon mustard

3 teaspoons cider vinegar

2 teaspoons golden caster sugar

3 tablespoons sunflower oil

3 tablespoons extra-virgin olive oil

1 small garlic clove, bruised

salt and freshly ground black pepper

First, make the dressing. Put all the ingredients, including the seasoning, in a clean jam jar or a small bowl, and shake or stir until thoroughly combined.

Cut the base from the lettuce and separate the leaves. Give them a good wash in cold water, taking care not to bruise them. Drain the leaves and then dry them in a salad spinner.

Slice the black pudding into thick 3cm (1¼in) rounds, then peel away the skin and discard. Heat the oil in a medium frying pan over a medium heat. Add the black pudding and fry, turning occasionally, for 7–8 minutes, until it starts to crisp around the edges. Remove the pan from the heat, then remove the black pudding from the pan and keep warm. Remove the crusts from the bread and tear each slice into rough, croûton-sized pieces. Place the pan back on the heat and add the butter. When it's bubbling away, throw in the bread pieces and fry, turning frequently, until crispy and golden on all sides. Season with a pinch of salt, sprinkle over the thyme leaves, then take the pan off the heat and set aside.

Place enough lettuce leaves for two people in a large bowl together with the sliced spring onions. Spoon over half the dressing and carefully turn the leaves to coat them.

Divide the lettuce and spring onion mixture equally between two large plates. Place the warm black pudding next to the leaves and scatter over the croûtons. Finish with an extra drizzle of dressing for each plate and serve.

Barbecued little gems with cucumber, white beans & tahini

I adore cooking lettuce. Sometimes, I like to wilt it with chicken stock and plenty of black pepper, parsley and lovage. Sometimes, I fry wedges of small lettuce in butter and olive oil, with salty anchovies and lots of garlic, until its sugars caramelize, then I serve it with heaps of grated Parmesan cheese. And soup, I make soup a lot with lettuce. But, with their close, tight leaves, little gem lettuces are also perfect for cooking on the barbecue or chargrilling. You want to get the embers good and hot, to give some real colour to the cut face of the lettuce. The contrast in this warm salad comes from the fresh, cool crunch of cucumber. It's all brought together with a beautiful, sort-of dressing, made from white beans, yoghurt and tahini.

SERVES 8 AS A STARTER
OR 4 AS A MAIN

3 tablespoons extra-virgin olive oil

2 garlic cloves, peeled and grated

1 x 400g (14oz) tin of white beans, such as cannellini or butter beans

juice and zest of 1 lemon

2 tablespoons tahini

4 tablespoons plain natural yoghurt

2 tablespoons chopped flat-leaf parsley leaves

4 little gem lettuces, halved, washed and patted dry

1 medium or 2 small firm cucumbers, halved lengthways and cut into 1.5cm (5/8in) slices

1 small bunch of chives, finely chopped and a few left whole

salt and black pepper

Heat 1 tablespoon of the olive oil in a medium frying pan over a medium–high heat, then add the garlic. Fry for 25–30 seconds, until the garlic begins to soften, then add the white beans and lemon zest. Stir to combine and cook for 1–2 minutes more, until the white beans are warmed through. Now, stir in the tahini, yoghurt, lemon juice and parsley, along with 2–3 tablespoons of water. Cook for a further 1–2 minutes, until spoonable. If it's too thick, add a little more water. Remove the pan from the heat.

Light your barbecue. Season the little gem halves with salt and pepper, and drizzle them with 1 tablespoon of the oil. When your barbecue coals are glowing nice and hot, lay your little gem lettuce, cut-sides down, onto the grill. Grill the lettuce for 5–10 minutes on each side – how long will depend upon the heat of your coals, but aim for the lettuce halves to soften, take on some colour, and caramelize; a little charring improves the dish. (Alternatively, cook on a preheated chargrill pan.) When the lettuce halves are ready, place them on a large serving platter cut-side up.

Put the bean and tahini dressing back on the heat to warm through, and give it a final stir. Spoon it over the lettuce, making sure it trickles through and around the layers of leaves. Scatter over the prepared cucumber, sprinkle with the chopped chives, strew over the long chives, then drizzle over the remaining olive oil and season everything with salt and pepper. Serve the salad straight away.

Lettuce salad with herbs & flowers

When I was younger I worked in a kitchen that served a 'mixed salad'. The chef taught me how to make it. He said, 'Put a handful of chopped iceberg in the bottom of this bowl. Then take a few slices of cucumber out of that tub of water and put them on top, then take a few strips of red pepper out of that tub of water and scatter those over the cucumber. That's it, okay?' The only thing I really agreed with was that the salad should go in a bowl. Still, in a funny way, that experience taught me more about making a salad than you might think. Sometimes you have to get lost to be found. Here are a few of my current thoughts on putting together a salad now that I've been lucky enough to cut and mix my own from the tended organic gardens at River Cottage. There, some lettuces are tight-hearted and bullet shaped; others are soft, open and nearly all water. The majority are light, sweet and clean in flavour, and there are some that are so scarily bitter they shake your mouth and rattle your teeth. None is unpleasant, variety is key.

There is no right or wrong in a mixed salad; there is no recipe – it's whatever appears on the day. All you need is a variety of fresh leaves that offer a balance of textures, a handful of your favourite fragrant herbs, and, if you can find them, a whisper of colourful flowers and petals.

At River Cottage, the hearted heads grow in rows beside the peppery, barbed orientals, the rockets and the thick, mottled-purple mustards that I love. These leaves give a salad swathes of character. I am able to cut bunches of green herbs (coriander and parsley are favourites). I add these when pert and full of life. When they are left alone, they bloom – a distillation of flavour and fragrance in the bud and petals of the plant. I particularly love flowering fennel and chives, but coriander and chervil flowers make punchy little additions, too. We also grow flowers specifically for our salads; they add colour, contrast and flavour. The sun-up yellow and sun-down orange of marigold is a favourite; as are the fire-red of nasturtium, and the cloud-white and lilac of borage.

There are other interesting things I like to add: young kale and chard leaves, particularly those from red Russian and rainbow varieties; small, tender sorrel leaves; young, raw agretti (monk's beard); and the uniquely peppery leaves from the nasturtium plant. Fresh carrot tops and tender mint leaves are both worth trying. Scattered cautiously, the smallest blades of wild garlic are pretty good, as are wild garlic flowers. And while we're on the wild theme, try hawthorn shoots and flowers, small, fleshy sea-beet leaves, chickweed, dandelion leaves, and even young yarrow.

If you can't grow your own herbs and leaves, buy them fresh from greengrocers, farm shops, allotments and direct from small-scale commercial growers. I find it best to wash the leaves and herbs carefully in a large bowl of very cold water soon after cutting. This is particularly important if it's warm outside, as leaves will begin to wilt straight away. Invest in a salad spinner and spin your leaves and herbs dry, then keep them in the fridge in a large bowl or deep tray covered with a damp, clean, light cloth. You don't need to wash the flowers (the water will damage the petals), just scatter them over your salad before you serve.

Gooseberries with smoked cod's roe & nasturtium leaves

I've always liked gooseberries and smoked mackerel together – a sharp gooseberry compote cuts through the richness of the oily fish and balances its smoky tones. I've drawn on the same principles for this smoked roe and gooseberry dish. Ask your fishmonger or at the supermarket fish counter for fresh, soft, smoked roe – it's best if it hasn't been frozen. The gooseberries should be ripe and sugary. I love the peppery tang of nasturtium leaves, reminiscent of horseradish. If you can't get hold of these, you could use peppery rocket or mustard leaf instead.

SERVES 2

100–150g (3½–5½oz) smoked cod's roe

1 handful of nasturtium leaves, or rocket

2 handfuls of ripe gooseberries, stalks removed

2 tablespoons extra-virgin olive oil

juice of ½ small lemon

salt and freshly ground black pepper

Place the cod's roe on a board and use a sharp knife to slice it into 2–3mm (1⁄16–1⁄8in) rounds. Divide these equally between two plates. Scatter over a handful of nasturtium or rocket leaves. Halve the larger gooseberries, or leave them whole if you prefer, then divide them equally between the plates, scattering them around the roe. Drizzle over the olive oil, pour over the lemon juice and season well with salt and pepper. Serve immediately with rye crisp breads (see p. 150) on the side.

Gooseberry & tarragon sorbet

This is sorbet at its most refreshing: it's sharp, almost sour, then honey-sweet. It's like a little fight kicking off in your mouth. Then, from nowhere, it's all aniseed – that's the effect of the tarragon, which is a beautiful herb to use in desserts, particularly sorbets and ices. (The sorbet works really well without it, too.) Riper berries give a sweeter sorbet, so add the sugar slowly, and taste before you churn. Reduce the amount of sugar by a few grammes to get the balance right, if you need to, but remember that the sweetness will be a little muted once the mixture is frozen.

SERVES 6–8

500g (1lb 2oz) ripe gooseberries

150g (5½oz) golden caster sugar

4 or 5 tarragon sprigs

FOR THE GOOSEBERRY TOPPING

2 handfuls of ripe gooseberries

1 squeeze of lemon juice

1 tablespoon golden caster sugar

a few tender tarragon sprigs, to serve (optional)

Place all the sorbet ingredients along with 150ml (5fl oz) water into a large heavy-based pan over a medium heat. Bring the contents up to a simmer, then place a lid on the pan. Cook for 8–10 minutes, until the gooseberries are broken down and soft. Remove from the heat and push the mixture through a sieve into a clean bowl. Allow to cool, then chill in the refrigerator completely – about 1–2 hours. Pour the mixture into an ice-cream machine and churn until soft set, then remove to a bowl or container, cover, and place in the freezer to firm up for at least 3–4 hours.

To make the gooseberry topping, slice any larger gooseberries in half, leaving the smaller ones whole. Place in a bowl, pour over the lemon juice and toss the gooseberries to coat, then sprinkle in the sugar and toss to coat again.

Before serving, remove the sorbet from the freezer and allow it to stand at room temperature for 10–15 minutes to soften slightly. Serve a couple of scoops of sorbet in each glass or onto each plate, spoon over a few sugary gooseberries from the topping mixture, then finish off with a tender sprig of tarragon, if you like. Serve straight away.

Lemon & gooseberry tart with elderflower fritters

Lemon, gooseberry and elderflower – even the words taste good. I can almost smell the dusty elderflower pollen, feel the bur of the gooseberries, and taste the lively citrus of lemon oil. I've made loads of different lemon tarts over the years, but none quite as simple as this one.

SERVES 8

1 quantity pastry (see p. 196), rolled out to 3–4mm (⅛–1⁄16in) thick

100g (3½oz) ripe gooseberries, halved

100g (3½oz) fragrant runny honey

juice of 1 large lemon (about 100ml/3½fl oz)

finely grated zest of 1 lemon

8 large egg yolks

50g (1¾oz) golden caster sugar

225g (8oz) unsalted butter, cubed and chilled, plus extra for greasing

FOR THE FRITTERS

20g (¾oz) cornflour

30g/1oz plain flour

sunflower oil, for deep frying

8 small elderflower heads

2–3 teaspoons golden caster sugar, for dusting the fritters

icing sugar, for dusting the tart (optional)

Heat your oven to 180°C/350°F/gas mark 4. Grease and flour an 18–20cm/7–8in tart tin. Lay the rolled pastry over the tart case, tucking it down into the corners (you'll have a little overhang). Refrigerate for 15–20 minutes, then remove from the fridge and line the case with baking parchment and baking beans. Place in the oven for 20 minutes, then take out the beans and parchment and blind bake the case for a further 10–15 minutes, until crisp and golden. Remove from the oven and trim around the edge to neaten.

To make the curd, place the gooseberries in a pan with 2–3 tablespoons water, over a medium heat. Bring to a gentle simmer and cook for 6–7 minutes, stirring regularly until the gooseberries are tender. Remove from the heat and pass the gooseberries through a sieve into a large heatproof bowl. Add the honey, lemon juice and zest, egg yolks and sugar. Whisk to combine.

Place the bowl over a pan of barely simmering water. Stir continuously and when the mixture has thickened and is hot, drop in the butter, a few cubes at a time, stirring to encourage it to melt. When you've incorporated all the butter, cook for 2–3 minutes, stir, then remove the bowl from the pan. Turn off the heat. Strain the curd through a sieve into a large bowl, then pour it into the tart case. Refrigerate for 6–8 hours, until set.

To make the fritters, combine the flour and cornflour with 3 tablespoons of water, and whisk until smooth. Fill a medium saucepan 5cm (2in) deep with sunflower oil. Place the oil over a high heat, then drip in a few drops of batter – if they fizz the oil is frying-hot. Dip the elderflower heads into the batter, shake them, then lower them one at a time into the oil. Fry each for 1 minute, or until crisp. Dust the fritters with caster sugar and serve on top of the tart, with a final dusting of icing sugar, if you wish.

orchard

orchard | Apple, bake, plum. A pudding, a sauce, all coarse and plump. Ripe like a kiss. Mist in the morning, baskets, clasping, shaking the bough. Make gentle slow, low sweets. Clear, bright jars of treats for your meats and your suppers. An autumn gale, a wassail, the press, the cheese in the cider shed. Scrumping for apples, two boys jump to the ground. Soft cakes, sugar wasps, Bramley, Laxton and Annie. Sheep graze, high-banked lanes, and the little gate that opens up the orchard.

apples

pears

quince

damsons

blackcurrants

Apple rye & cider cake

This apple cake is made with rye flour, which gives it a nutty, wholesome flavour. I also add a generous glass of cider and some thyme leaves, which work beautifully well with the rye taste.

SERVES 8–10

400g (14oz) cooking apples, peeled, cored and cubed

juice and zest of 1 lemon

150g (5½oz) butter, diced and softened, plus extra for greasing

200g (7oz) light brown soft sugar

3 eggs, beaten

100ml (3½fl oz) cider

150g (5½oz) plain flour

100g (3½oz) rye flour

2 teaspoons baking powder

pinch of salt

3 thyme sprigs, leaves picked

2 small dessert apples

2 tablespoons demerara sugar

Heat the oven to 160°C/315°F/gas mark 2–3.

Toss the cooking apples with the lemon juice and zest and set aside. Grease and line with baking parchment the base and sides of a 24cm (9½in) diameter springform cake tin. Beat the butter and light brown soft sugar together until light and pale. You can do this by hand, but it's easier with an electric mixer. Add the beaten egg, a little at a time until it's all incorporated, then trickle in the cider, stirring continuously. Sift the flours and baking powder together with the pinch of salt into a separate bowl, then fold this into the butter-and-egg mixture, followed by the chopped lemony cooking apple and the thyme leaves. Fold together to combine.

Spoon the cake batter into the prepared tin. Peel, quarter, core and thinly slice the dessert apples, and arrange the slices in a single layer around the edge of the cake. Finally, sprinkle with the demerara sugar.

Bake in the centre of the oven for 50–60 minutes or until a skewer inserted into the centre of the cake comes out clean. Transfer the cake to a wire rack to cool before serving in slices. Once cool, the unsliced cake will keep in an airtight container for 3–4 days.

Fried apples with sage, pig's cheek & celeriac

I love this plate of food. It's rustic and humble, but it's got everything I could hope for. Pig's cheek is delicious, so if you haven't had it before, I'd urge you to give it a go. I always use the whole cheek, rather than the dark middle chunk of meat, sometimes sold as the 'cushion'. The whole cheek offers much more. You'll need to brine it two days before you want to serve the dish.

SERVES 2

300g (10½oz) fine sea salt

1 free-range or organic whole pig's cheek

1 onion, quartered

2 carrots, peeled and roughly chopped

2 celery sticks, roughly chopped

2 bay leaves

½ small celeriac, peeled and cubed

1 knob of butter

2 dessert apples, such as russet or Cox, cored and cut into wedges

1 bunch of small sage leaves

1 thyme sprig

salt and freshly ground black pepper

First, make a brine. Find a large plastic bowl. Add the sea salt and 1 litre (35fl oz) of water and whisk well until the salt dissolves. Submerge the pig's cheek in the brine and refrigerate for 48 hours.

To cook, remove the cheek from the brine, rinse it, then place it in a large heavy-based pan with the onion, carrots, celery and bay leaves. Cover with water, place the pan on a high heat and bring the liquid to a simmer. Reduce the heat to low and cook gently, uncovered, for 2½–3 hours or until the cheek meat and skin are tender. Remove the whole cheek and set aside to cool, then refrigerate. Pour the stock through a sieve into a clean bowl, cover the stock, allow to cool, then refrigerate that, too.

Skim the majority of the fat from the top of the chilled stock. Place the celeriac in a heavy-based pan. Pour over enough of the liquid stock to cover the celeriac and place it on a high heat. Bring to a simmer, then allow it to simmer gently for 20–30 minutes, until the celeriac is tender. Use a slotted spoon to remove the celeriac from the pan into a food processor. Spoon over just a little stock, add the butter, then blitz until smooth. Season to taste.

Place a large frying pan on a medium–high heat. Slice the cooked cheek into 2 thick or 4 thinner slices. (Reserve any leftovers for another day – they're great fried until crisp and scattered over lettuce and boiled eggs.) Fry the cheek for 3–4 minutes on each side, or until golden and heated through. Set aside. Add the apples to the pan along with a little salt and pepper, the sage leaves and thyme sprigs and fry, turning the apples in the well-flavoured pork fat, for 1–2 minutes until lightly caramelized at the edges.

Spoon the celeriac equally between two bowls, then add some fried apples and sage and the crispy cheek slices. Serve immediately.

Apple, greengage & pumpkin-seed salad

Do you know what happens when you dress apples in lots of lemon juice? It brings out a secret flavour in them, a beautiful flavour that I can never quite place. It's somewhere between roses and cicely, I think, but I can't be sure. Greengages are small plums. They're juicy and sweet and work really well with the crunch of the apple. I've added toasted pumpkin seeds to this recipe, and fresh tarragon — a brilliant herb to use with apples.

SERVES 2

2 dessert apples

juice of ½ lemon

8 ripe greengages, or other ripe plums

1 large tarragon sprig, leaves picked

2 tablespoons pumpkin seeds

2 teaspoons runny honey

2 tablespoons extra-virgin olive oil

pinch of salt

Using a sharp paring knife or a mandoline, slice the apples into rounds as thinly as you can — ideally about 1–2mm (⅟₃₂–⅟₁₆) thick. Remove the pips from the slices as necessary (you don't need to remove the core — it's totally edible).

Divide the apple slices equally between two large plates, then drizzle over half the lemon juice.

Slice the greengages or plums into 1–3mm (⅟₃₂–⅛in) slices and scatter them over the apple. Tear over the tarragon leaves, sprinkle over the pumpkin seeds, and drizzle over the honey and olive oil. Trickle a little of the remaining lemon juice over each plate and finish off with a tiny pinch of salt.

Fried pears with roast red onions & crisped puy lentils

This colourful, early autumn salad is so easy. Sometimes all you need to make a lovely supper are three well-matched ingredients. Choose ripe pears, but not overripe, as you want them to fry in the hot pan without their breaking up too much. My obsession with crispy lentils began at River Cottage, and I'm loving them lots right now. We must love them together, because they are just outrageously good, and here lend real crunch.

SERVES 4–6

100g (3½oz) puy lentils, rinsed

2 red onions, each cut into 8 wedges

4 tablespoons extra-virgin olive oil

2 ripe pears

1 knob of butter

juice of ½ lemon

salt and freshly ground black pepper

Heat the oven to 180°C/350°C/gas mark 4. Put the rinsed lentils in a medium pan, cover with water and set over a high heat. Bring to a simmer, then cook for 18–25 minutes, until the lentils have softened but retain some bite. Drain them, then leave them in the colander and allow the steam to evaporate.

Meanwhile, place the onion wedges in a roasting tray with 2 tablespoons of the olive oil, toss to coat, and season with plenty of salt and pepper. Roast the onion in the oven for 25–30 minutes, or until the wedges are soft and starting to colour. Remove from the oven and set aside.

Slice each pear into quarters, remove the cores, then cut each quarter in half again, giving 16 wedges of pear altogether. Heat the butter and 1 tablespoon of the remaining oil in a large frying pan over a medium heat. When the butter and oil mixture is bubbling, add the pear slices to the pan. Fry them gently for 3–5 minutes on each side, or until they have taken on a little colour. Remove the pear wedges from the pan and keep them warm.

Leaving the frying pan on the hob, increase the heat to medium–high. Add the remaining oil, followed by the cooked lentils. Season with a little salt and pepper, and fry, tossing regularly, for 15–20 minutes, or until the lentils are crisped.

Arrange the warm roast onions and pears on a large serving platter. Scatter over the lentils, drizzle over the lemon juice, and bring to the table straight away.

Pears with crisped kale & lardo

This interesting combination works well because everything is so perfectly different. Make sure the pears are at their most ripe, so that they are full to bursting. The kale should be as dry as bone, the definition of brittle; and the lardo, pure fat — both salty and sweet and unbelievably buttery — should be cold. Together, these ingredients make an extremely balanced and delicious salad. If you find lardo a little too extreme, try a lovely cured pancetta instead.

SERVES 2

100g (3½oz) curly kale, stripped of any thick stalk

2 tablespoons extra-virgin olive oil

2 ripe pears

8–12 very thin slices lardo or cured well-marbled pancetta

2 teaspoons runny honey

3 or 4 thyme sprigs, leaves stripped and lightly bruised

juice of ½ lemon

salt and freshly ground black pepper

Heat the oven to 120°C/235°F/gas mark 1.

First, make the crisped kale. Wash the kale, then spin it in a salad spinner until it's really dry. Tear the leaves into large pieces and place them in a bowl with 1 tablespoon of the olive oil and a good pinch of salt.

Using your hands, mix the leaves well to coat in the oil. Line a baking tray with baking parchment, then arrange the kale in an even layer on the tray and place it in the oven. Bake for 25–30 minutes, turning the individual leaves once or twice during cooking, until they are nice and crisp. Remove the leaves from the oven and allow to cool.

Divide the cooled, crisped kale equally between two shallow bowls. Quarter and core the pears and tuck them in between the kale leaves, again dividing them equally between the two bowls.

Drape 4–6 slices of lardo or pancetta over and around the kale and pears on each plate, then trickle over the honey, the remaining olive oil, some thyme leaves and a drizzle of lemon juice. Season lightly and take to the table immediately.

Pears cooked in elderberries & juniper

There are a lot of elder trees growing in my garden – they look so magnificent, particularly when the sprays are heavy with tender, dark berries. These berries are so underrated; I always wonder how else I can use them. In this recipe I poach some pears in the same way I always do – gently and with plenty of aromatics – but also pack as many elderberry heads in the pan as I can fit. As the pears cook, the berries give up, break and burst, staining the pears a vivid red-purple. The colour is more intense than that of blood and its tones deeper than blackberry. When I taste the poaching liquor, it's more than I hoped for: the juniper and bay are heady and strong; the elder is tannin and honey, and thick with body. The poaching liquor makes a wonderful syrup to serve with the pears. Alternatively, you can strain it, bottle it and use it as a cordial; or, if you're feeling adventurous, sweeten it and churn it into the most incredible sorbet.

SERVES 4

4 large medium–ripe pears

1 large bowl of ripe elderberry heads, plus 4 good-looking heads to serve

200g (7oz) golden caster sugar

12 juniper berries, bruised

4 bay leaves

pared zest of 1 lemon

Peel the pears as carefully as possible – you want them to retain their lovely shape – and place them in a medium pan with the elderberry heads, sugar, juniper berries, bay leaves, lemon zest and 500ml (17fl oz water). Place the pan over a medium heat and bring the liquid up to a simmer. Cook gently, for about 25 minutes, pressing the elderberries against the side of the pan with a wooden spoon (you want to encourage them to break down and give up their colour and flavour) as the liquid simmers away, until the pears are tender. When the pears yield easily to the point of a knife, remove the pan from the heat, then lift the pears out of the pan using a slotted spoon and set aside on a plate to cool. Reserve the cooking syrup.

When you're ready to serve, place a large frying pan over a medium heat. Add 3–4 tablespoons of the pear cooking syrup and bring the liquid up to a simmer. Set the 4 good-looking elderberry heads berries downwards in the pan and cook for 1–2 minutes, or until they are just starting to burst and the liquor has reduced and thickened slightly. Remove the pan from the heat. Cut the cooled pears in half. Place 2 pear halves on each plate and set a head of bursting elderberries next to them. Spoon over the fragrant syrup and serve straight away.

Quince tarte Tatin

I've made quite a few tartes Tatin, and every time it feels exciting. It's 'the reveal' that I look forward to the most – that point of jeopardy, when you invert the pan onto a plate before serving. Sweet dessert apples are the classic fruit to use for tarte Tatin, of course, but here I've used quince, which works beautifully with sprigs of fresh thyme and star anise in the pan. I've made lovely versions with pears, too, as well as savoury: parsnip tarte Tatin is delicious served with a few crisped onions, some hot mustard, and crème fraîche; beetroot tarte Tatin is sweet and earthy and perfect served with warm slices of fresh goat's cheese and toasted walnuts.

SERVES 4

4 medium–large quinces, peeled, quartered and cored

2 knobs of butter

75g (2½oz) light brown soft sugar

2 star anise

4–6 thyme sprigs

200g (7oz) all-butter puff pastry

Cut each quince quarter into 3 or 4 wedges, each about 1cm (½in) thick at the outer edge. Place a large frying pan over a medium heat. Melt the butter in the pan, then add the sugar and 1 tablespoon of water. When everything starts to bubble, add the quince pieces. Cook the quince for 15–20 minutes, turning the wedges very gently so as not to break them up, but helping to ensure they cook evenly and equally, until they're almost tender.

Meanwhile, heat the oven to 180°C/350°F/gas mark 4. When the quince is ready, remove the pan from the heat and scoop out the cooked wedges onto a plate to cool a little, reserving the caramel in the pan. Add the star anise and thyme sprigs to the pan, keeping it off the heat. When the quince is cool enough to handle, place the cooked wedges back in the pan, arranging them carefully to make two concentric circles of quince slices, beginning in the centre of the tart. Press the wedges down lightly into the pan.

Roll out the pastry to 3mm (⅛in) thick and cut it into a circle that will fit snugly over your quince pieces. Lay it over, gently tucking in the pastry edges around the inside edge of the pan. Bake the tart in the oven for 30–35 minutes, until the pastry is well risen and golden, then remove the pan from the oven. Allow the tart to rest in the pan for 10–15 minutes, then place a plate over the pan and in one quick, flipping motion, invert the tart onto the plate. Carefully lift away the pan for your reveal! Serve the tarte Tatin immediately with double cream, vanilla ice cream, or custard on the side.

Fried pheasant with quince & bay

This rustic dish has an air of autumn about it. I like to think it's got all the colour and patina of a hedgerow as its greens turn to soft, mottled yellows and light, earthy browns. The first pheasant of the season usually coincides nicely with the quince harvest. You can prepare the quince well in advance – once cooled, it keeps beautifully in the fridge in its cooking syrup. If you're not having pheasant, you can just as easily serve the quince alongside some good cheese and cold ham, or enjoy it sweet – with vanilla ice cream.

SERVES 2

pared zest of ½ lemon

8 black peppercorns

2 bay leaves

1 teaspoon fennel seeds (optional)

2 thyme sprigs

75g (2½oz) sugar

2 tablespoons runny honey

2 quinces, peeled, quartered and cored

1 tablespoon extra-virgin olive oil

75g (2½oz) unsmoked bacon lardons

2 pheasant or guinea fowl breasts (about 150g/5½oz each)

1 knob of butter

salt and freshly ground black pepper

First, make a fragrant syrup. Place the lemon zest, peppercorns, bay leaves, fennel seeds (if using), thyme sprigs, sugar, honey and 300ml (10½fl oz) water in a medium pan. Place the pan over a medium heat and bring up to a gentle simmer.

Cut each quince quarter into 2 or 3 more evenly sized wedges. Place the wedges into the simmering syrup and cook very gently for 25–45 minutes, until the wedges are tender. (The cooking time can vary from quince to quince.) When the quince are ready, remove from the heat, then use a slotted spoon to take them out of the pan and set aside.

Heat the olive oil in a large frying pan over a medium heat. Add the lardons and fry, stirring regularly, for 4–6 minutes, or until the lardons are beginning to colour a little. Season the pheasant or guinea fowl breasts with salt and pepper and add them to the pan together with the cooked quince. Cook the breasts for 2–3 minutes on each side, or until golden brown and cooked to your liking, and until the quince wedges are lightly caramelized. Remove the pan from the heat, then remove the breasts from the pan and set aside to rest.

Divide the lardons and quince wedges equally between two warmed plates. Then place the frying pan over a high heat and add 100ml (3½fl oz) of the fragrant syrup (save the rest to use as a fruit syrup). Reduce this by half, take the pan off the heat and stir in the butter until melted; season to taste. Cut each breast into thick slices and divide it equally between the two plates, arranging it next to the quince. Spoon over the syrup and serve straight away.

Quince cheese

Quince cheese is one of my favourite things to make with this fragrant fruit, preserving all its amazing texture and perfume for months to come. The cheese has the most enchanting deep-red colour, a result of the slow and gentle cooking process. It makes a delicious accompaniment to actual cheese, especially (and famously) Spanish manchego, or a ripe, blue-veined cheese, or a soft goat's or sheep's cheese. You can also try it with roast meats, such as pheasant or chicken, or with baked ham. I quite often melt a spoonful into gravy to give it a fruity sweetness.

MAKES 3–4 LARGE
JAM JARS

1kg (2lb 4oz) quince, roughly chopped

about 500g (1lb 2oz) granulated sugar

Place the fruit into a large heavy-based saucepan or preserving pan and cover with water, so that the waterline sits a few centimetres/ an inch or so above the line of the fruit. Place the pan on a high heat and bring the water up to a simmer. Place the lid on the pan, turn down the heat and simmer for about 60 minutes, until the fruit is soft and broken down and you're left with something approaching a fruit pulp. (If you don't have a lid, don't worry – just keep an eye on the amount of water in the pan and top up if you need to.)

Once the fruit is cooked, remove the pan from the heat and allow it to stand for 30 minutes or so. Then, place a sturdy sieve over a bowl and tip the pulp out of the pan into the sieve. Use the back of a ladle to force the pulp through the sieve into the bowl. Alternatively, you can put the pulp through a mouli, if you have one.

Weigh the contents of the bowl and add two-thirds of that weight in granulated sugar. Clean the cooking pan, and then return the sweetened quince mixture to it. Set it over a medium heat and bring it up to a simmer, stirring or whisking regularly for about 60 minutes or more, until the mixture has thickened so that a wooden spoon dragged through it reveals the base of the pan for a couple of seconds before the mixture comes together again. It may begin to bubble, but keep stirring and it won't burn. Don't rush.

Pour the quince into sterilized jars (see p. 144) and seal. Store in a cool place (it will keep for several months) until you're ready to use it.

Damson ice cream

There is a damson tree in the square of the nearby village. The fruit is bruise blue-and-black with silver-dusted skin. By the end of the season much of the fruit is blemished, split or scarred, but that makes it no less ripe and sweet. It's these less-perfect damsons that I use to make ice cream – something I've done at River Cottage every year. The result is a soft shade of purple with a sugar-muffled sharpness – a great balance. I'll often serve one or two whole, ripe damsons alongside the ice cream.

SERVES 12

500g (1lb 2oz) ripe damsons, plus extra for serving (optional)

6 egg yolks

200g (7oz) golden caster sugar

300ml (10½fl oz) double cream

200ml (7fl oz) whole milk

Place the whole damsons in a large heavy-based pan with 3 tablespoons of water over a medium heat. Give the fruit a good shake and place a lid on the pan. Bring up to a simmer, then reduce the heat to cook gently for 10–12 minutes until the damsons have broken down completely. Place a fine sieve over a bowl and pass the softened damsons through the sieve, encouraging them through with the back of a wooden spoon, if necessary, to create a purée. Set aside while you make the custard.

To make the custard, place the egg yolks in a bowl with the sugar. Put the cream and milk in a small pan over a medium heat. When the cream comes up to a simmer pour it into the bowl over the yolks, whisking all the time. Pour the egg and cream mixture into a clean medium pan over a low heat and cook gently, whisking continuously without letting the custard boil, until it begins to thicken. Pass the hot custard through a sieve into the bowl of damson purée and whisk well to combine, then allow to cool.

Pour the damson–custard mixture into an ice-cream machine and churn until soft set. Transfer the ice-cream to a suitable container, cover, and place in the freezer for at least 3–4 hours to firm up.

Remove the ice-cream from the freezer 15–20 minutes before you intend to serve it. I like it served on its own, or with just one or two fresh, ripe damsons alongside.

Damsons with sage, Camembert & cacao

Fruity, sharp damsons, with their chutney-like qualities, make the ideal accompaniment to a strong, ripe cheese such as Camembert. The honey in this recipe sweetens the fruit just enough to balance their acidity, while the cacao nibs (which are simply unprocessed cocoa beans, broken into little bits) offer texture, their bittersweet character matching incredibly well with the sage. I like to serve this colourful combination as a cheese course, perhaps with a small cup of good coffee, freshly brewed.

SERVES 2

1 tablespoon extra-virgin olive oil

1 small knob of butter

2–3 teaspoons runny honey

8 ripe damsons, halved and stoned

12 small sage leaves

125g (4½oz) ripe Camembert or Brie

2 teaspoons cacao nibs

salt and freshly ground black pepper

Take the cheese out of the fridge and allow it to come up to room temperature while you cook the damsons.

Place a medium pan over a medium heat, add the olive oil, butter and honey and when hot and bubbling add the damson halves, cut side down. Tear in most of the sage leaves and cook the fruit for 3–4 minutes on the first side, then carefully turn the damson halves over and cook for 2–3 minutes on the other side, or until the fruits are tender but still just holding their shape. Remove from the heat and allow to cool in the pan.

Slice the cheese and divide the slices equally between each plate. Top with equal servings of damsons, a few of the torn sage leaves and a good trickle of the buttery, sweet pan juices. Finish with a light sprinkling of cacao nibs and a little salt and pepper. Serve straight away.

Crackling & damsons

I have this idea in my mind, like an imprecise memory: I've been walking with friends, along a high and long stretch of Dorset coastline. The footpaths that skirt the sheer fall to the ocean are kept trim by hardy sheep. It's autumn, the wind is strong but not cold; the sky is grey, but no rain falls. Gulls and ravens swing east and west on the up-draft. A little kestrel hangs still above the bracken, then plummets. It begins to rain, but in the near distance the pub looks warm. We go in and order pints of light ales and some whiskey. The owner brings out crackling with a damson compote. (This recipe is my attempt to make that idea a reality.)

SERVES 4

400–500g (14oz–1lb 2oz) pork skin from the shoulder or loins, with 1cm (½in) fat on its underside

salt

FOR THE COMPOTE

300g (10½oz) ripe damsons, halved and stoned

50g (1¾oz) sugar

1 star anise

1 small bunch of thyme sprigs, leaves picked

1 dried chilli (optional)

To get the best crackling, it's really important that the pork skin is dry to the touch. Keep it uncovered on the bottom shelf of the fridge overnight, or even for a couple of days before you begin.

When you're ready to cook, heat the oven to 230–240°C/450–475°F/gas mark 8. Then, make the compote. Place the damson halves in a medium pan with the sugar, star anise, thyme leaves, dried chilli (if using) and 2–3 tablespoons water. Bring the contents of the pan to a gentle simmer, stirring once or twice, for 3–5 minutes, until the damsons bleed and start to break down. Remove from the heat, gently stir, then leave the damson mixture to cool in the pan.

Place the dry pig skin, fat-side down on a board. Take a super-sharp knife and cut the skin into 2–3cm (¾–1¼in) strips. Place a metal rack over a roasting tray and lay the strips of skin on top, fat-side down. Season all over with salt, then place in the oven for 15–20 minutes, until the crackling is puffed and popped, light and golden. If it's not quite there after this time, turn down the oven to 180°C/350°F/gas mark 4 and cook for a further 10–15 minutes, or until you think it's looking great.

Remove the crackling from the oven and lift it off the tray onto a board or serving platter. Save the rendered fat in the tray (for roast potatoes another day).

Serve the damson compote in a bowl or in the pan with a pile of crackling on the side, for dipping and scooping.

Blackcurrant greens with chilli, ginger & garlic

I try to keep some shape and texture to a handful of the blackcurrants when I make this simple (yet surprisingly full-on) dressing – the acidity of the tart little berries takes the place of vinegar. Served with boiled brown or white rice, this dish makes a gorgeous and invigorating lunch; or, on its own, it makes a smart accompaniment to roast duck or spiced roast pork belly. Silky rainbow chard works beautifully here, as does cavolo nero (a brilliant variety of kale), although the dressing is the business turned through any fresh seasonal greens.

SERVES 2 AS A SIDE

100g (3½oz) blackcurrants

1 large or 2 small garlic cloves, peeled and thinly sliced

½ small medium–hot chilli, deseeded and thinly sliced

3 cm (1¼in) piece root ginger, peeled and grated

2 teaspoons runny honey

1 tablespoon tamari or soy sauce

enough fresh greens, such as kale or chard or a mixture of both, to fill a colander

Remove the stalks and papery base from the blackcurrants so they are all ready to cook. Place them in a small pan with the sliced garlic and chilli, grated ginger, honey, tamari or soy sauce, and 2 teaspoons of water.

Place the pan over a low heat and bring the contents to a gentle simmer. Cook for 3–4 minutes, or until the blackcurrants are just starting to give up their juice but retain some of their form. Stir once or twice – it should have a thickish consistency that coats the spoon as you stir. Remove from the heat and set aside.

Bring a larger pan full of fresh, salted water to the boil. Prepare the greens by washing them and stripping off any excess stalk. Plunge the leaves into the boiling water and simmer for 3–5 minutes, or until they are cooked to your liking. Drain them well, then lift them, steaming, into a serving bowl. Spoon over the blackcurrant sauce and bring to the table straight away.

Blackcurrant & thyme ladyfingers

A pot full of blackcurrants cooked gently, just to bursting, with sugar and lots of fresh thyme is a proper treat. Cooled and spooned over vanilla ice cream or alongside a soft pannacotta... oh yeah! I don't know why thyme and blackcurrants go so well together, some science at work. These delicate biscuits are a playful example of this great combination. They are as light in the mouth as whipped milk or smoke, and are beautiful eaten while still warm. The little berries pop and bleed as they bake, which makes them completely irresistible.

MAKES 12

1 egg, separated

pinch of salt

½ teaspoon vanilla extract

30g (1oz) golden caster sugar

20g (¾oz) plain flour

100g (3½oz) ripe blackcurrants

2 thyme sprigs, leaves picked

2 tablespoons icing sugar

Heat the oven to 180°C/350°F/gas mark 4. If you're making your biscuits using a moulded tin, grease it lightly with butter; otherwise line a baking sheet with baking parchment.

Place the egg yolk, salt, vanilla and half of the sugar into a small bowl. Whisk for about 3–4 minutes, until light and thick. In a separate, larger bowl, use a clean whisk to whisk the egg white until it forms stiff peaks. Add the remaining sugar to the white, and whisk again until firm.

Add a tablespoon of the egg whites to the yolk mix, and gently use a rubber spatula to combine fully. Then, add the yolk mix to the remaining egg whites, sieve in the flour and, again using the spatula, gently fold everything together until evenly coloured.

Gently place the mixture into a piping bag, taking care not to knock out the air, and pipe the mixture either into your mould or onto the baking parchment in lines about 10cm (4in) long. Divide the blackcurrants randomly throughout the batters, pressing them down lightly with your fingers, then sprinkle over the thyme. Sprinkle with half the icing sugar, then leave to rest for 5 minutes. Sprinkle over the remaining icing sugar, and immediately place the biscuits in the oven. Bake for 12–15 minutes, until golden and fragrant, then remove from the oven and leave to cool. (If you've used a mould, remove the biscuits from it as soon as you take them out of the oven and allow them to cool on a wire rack.) The biscuits will keep for up to 2 days in an airtight container.

Blackcurrant cordial

This cordial makes me feel like I've caught the essence of late summer and I'm keeping it – hidden – preserved in a bottle. You can double or triple this recipe if you're growing your own blackcurrants, or if you've been to a farm to pick your own and have a glut to use up.

MAKES ABOUT 1 LITRE

600g (1lb 5oz) ripe blackcurrants

350g (12oz) golden caster or granulated sugar

2 teaspoons thyme leaves (optional)

juice and zest of 1 lemon

Give the blackcurrants a quick wash and remove their stalks, as usual, but don't worry about the papery little base if they have it. Place the blackcurrants, sugar, thyme (if using) and 500ml (17fl oz) water into a heavy-based large pan and place over a low heat, stirring continuously for about 5 minutes, until the sugar has completely dissolved.

Turn up the heat and bring the liquid to a simmer, uncovered, for 8–10 minutes, until the blackcurrants are soft to bursting, then add the lemon juice and zest and remove from the heat to cool in the pan.

Line a sieve with muslin cloth, or use a jelly bag, and place it over a jug or bowl. Pass the cooled fruit mixture through the lined sieve or the jelly bag, allowing it to drain into the bowl or jug for at least 1 hour (2 hours would be better). Encourage as much juice through as possible by pressing the pulp with the back of a spoon every now and then.

Pour the cordial from the bowl or jug into sterilized glass bottles (you can sterilize them by running through your dishwasher on its highest setting), seal the tops, and refrigerate. The cordial will keep for 3–4 weeks.

To serve, place a few ice cubes in a glass, pour over a little of the cordial, and top up with still or fizzy water to taste.

field

field | Sometimes the fields seem to move like the surface of warm water. The last dry breeze of summer. Distant stacks smoke, barley and rye. Everything is biscuit and dust. We run the tyre track mazes before the cut. The harvest is sweet with the humming thrash and turn of the machines at dusk. Windows, we begin to stand this side of you and look at each other again. Walks, the air holds us in its blue, then lets us go in ochre. Everything turns. The plough turns, the soil is thick and dark as night. The wheat flour in my hands is white.

rye

oats

wheat

barley

corn

Rye crackers

The fermenting leaven in these crackers gives them a really good flavour and a unique, brittle texture. Feel free to customize the cracker as you like. Here, I use caraway seed, because I love that flavour with rye, but sesame, linseed, poppy or sunflower would be really nice, too. The crackers are perfect with cheese, or with a delicate parfait and a little fruit jelly, or with something pickled. They keep well in an airtight container for several days.

SERVES 4–6

150g (5½oz) active rye starter (see below)

100g (3½oz) light rye flour, plus extra for scattering

1 teaspoon fine sea salt

1 tablespoon caraway seeds

FOR THE RYE STARTER

A rye starter is fermentation of flour and water. It contains natural, 'wild' yeasts and lactic acid bacteria. The wild yeasts produce carbon dioxide as well as alcohol, to make your bread rise. The bacteria help to give your bread its complex flavour. I use wholemeal rye flour because it seems to produce the most active starter; I also love its sweet nutty flavour. To make your own starter follow the steps below:

DAY 1 Place 25g (1oz rye) flour with 50ml (1¾fl oz) warm water in a clean bowl. Stir well, cover and leave overnight in a warm place (ideally at a temperature of around 30°C/86°F).

DAYS 2, 3 AND 4 Every day add a further 25g (1oz) rye flour and 50ml (1¾fl oz) warm water to the existing mix. After each addition, stir well, cover and set aside in the same warm place. (By Day 3 the mixture should be showing signs of fermentation.)

DAY 5 You should now have 300g (10½oz) or so of active rye starter, which you can now use in your baking. Keep the mixture in the fridge when you're not using it, but make sure to feed it once or twice, each time adding a further 25g (1oz) rye flour and 50ml (1¾fl oz) warm water, to ensure it's active before using again. Each time you use a quantity of active starter in your baking, replace its weight with a mixture of fresh flour and water in a ratio of 1 part flour to 2 parts water, and allow it to ferment for next time.

Place the rye starter, the flour and about 80–100ml (2½fl oz–3½fl oz) water in a bowl and beat well with a wooden spoon until thick – the mixture should be the consistency of very thick batter or very sticky dough. Cover, and leave to ferment in a warm place for 2–3 hours.

Heat the oven to 120°C/235°F/gas mark 1. Line a large, flat 35 x 35cm/14 x 14in (or equivalent rectangular) baking tray with baking parchment or, better still, with a non-stick silicone mat.

Using a spatula or palette knife, spread the cracker mixture out as evenly and thinly as you can over the parchment or mat. Bring it right up to the edges. Scatter over the salt, caraway seeds and a generous extra shake of rye flour. Bake in the oven for 45–50 minutes, until firm to the touch.

Remove the tray from the oven and use a palette knife or spatula to carefully lift the cracker from the parchment or silicone mat, easing it away in one piece.

Return the cracker to the oven, this time directly on the oven shelf, for a further 20 minutes, until it appears quite brittle. If it's not brittle after this time, pop it back in the oven and check it every 4–5 minutes until it is. Then, remove it from the oven and allow it to cool.

To serve, either bring the cracker to the table whole for your guests to crack and snap as required; or break it up and serve it in smaller pieces.

Dark rye bread with coriander seed & caraway

We make this bread at home once or twice a week. There's no kneading, no dough machine, no yeast — you simply need a few moments of your time to combine the ingredients, and then you just leave the dough to rise. With its lovely sticky texture and complex character, it's the best rye sourdough I've ever eaten. The seeds and the rye flour make it sweet and nutty, the coriander makes it zesty and the caraway makes it clean. Brilliant for sandwiches — particularly the kind of Scandinavian open sandwich you might find topped with some smoked fish, crème fraîche, chopped eggs and dill pickles — it's amazing toasted, too. Try it thickly spread with some cold, salted butter and finished off with a layer of good marmalade.

MAKES 1 LOAF

250g (9oz) active rye starter (see p. 150)

350g (12oz) light rye flour, plus extra for dusting and scattering

125g (4½oz) cooked pearl barley

1 tablespoon molasses

2–3 teaspoons coriander seeds

2–3 teaspoons caraway seeds

1–2 tablespoons sunflower seeds

1–2 tablespoons linseeds

10g (¼oz) fine sea salt

oil, for greasing

Pour the active rye starter into a large mixing bowl. Tip in all the remaining ingredients, except the oil, with about 200ml (7fl oz) water. Use a wooden spoon or your hands to work everything together into a loose dough.

Grease a 1kg (2lb 4oz) non-stick loaf tin with a little oil, then dust it liberally with rye flour. Using wet hands, form the dough into a loaf shape to sit loosely inside the tin, smoothing the dough's surface as best you can. Lower the dough into the prepared tin. Scatter the top with more rye flour, allowing some to fall around the sides of the dough, inside the tin — this will help prevent sticking and also give the surface of your bread a lovely aesthetic.

Place the tin in a clean plastic bag and leave the dough to prove in a warm place for 4–8 hours. As long as your rye starter was lively, the dough should rise to fill the tin.

When it's looking good, heat your oven to 200°C/400°F/gas mark 6. Place the tin on the middle shelf and bake the bread for 25 minutes, then turn down the heat to 180°C/350°F/gas mark 4 and bake for a further 20 minutes, until the loaf is risen and dark and sounds hollow when tapped.

Remove the loaf from the oven and turn it out onto a cooling rack. Allow it to settle for at least 1 hour before slicing. The loaf will be good for at least a week, if not 10 days.

Chocolate rye brownies with bay & almonds

Rye flour and good chocolate are extraordinarily delicious together. I often use rye in place of a plain flour in my baking – it brings its delicate roasted, nutty notes to chocolate cakes, fondants and biscuits, and plays off the bitter qualities of dark chocolate in a new and wonderful way. These rye brownies also contain aromatic bay, which accentuates and permeates the chocolate-and-rye marriage with its distinct perfume. A crunchy, sugary almond topping finishes off the brownies with an amazing extra texture.

SERVES 8–10

200g (7oz) good-quality dark chocolate, at least 70 per cent cocoa solids, broken into pieces

180g (6¼oz) unsalted butter, cubed and chilled, plus extra for greasing

2 pinches of fine sea salt

4 eggs

100g (3½oz) golden caster sugar

80g (2¾oz) soft brown sugar

150g (5½oz) light rye flour, plus extra for dusting

100g (3½oz) whole, skin-on almonds

finely grated zest of ½ orange

50g (1¾oz) golden granulated sugar

6–8 bay leaves

Heat the oven to 160°C/315°F/gas mark 2–3.

Grease and lightly flour a medium baking tin (about 20 x 30cm/ 8 x 12in). Melt the chocolate pieces and butter, with 1 pinch of the salt, in a large heatproof bowl set over a pan of very gently simmering water for 6–8 minutes, stirring once or twice, until the chocolate is smooth and delicious-looking. (Don't let the bowl touch the water.)Remove the bowl from the heat and set aside.

Separate 1 egg. Divide the white in half as best you can. In a large bowl, use an electric whisk to beat the remaining eggs, as well as the yolk and ½ egg white of the separated egg, with both the sugars until light, airy, pale and fluffy. Reserve the remaining ½ egg white.

Beat the whisked egg mixture into the melted chocolate mixture, then fold in the rye flour until the batter is fully combined. Pour the batter into the prepared tin.

To make the topping, whisk the reserved egg white in a bowl until light and airy, then fold in the almonds, orange zest, granulated sugar and remaining pinch of salt. Tumble together until the almonds are well-coated and the mixture is fully combined.

Spoon the almond topping evenly over the brownies, then dot the bay leaves over the top, pushing the base of each leaf a little way into the batter. Bake the brownies for 20–25 minutes, until they are cracked and firm on top, but gooey in the middle. Remove from the oven and leave to cool completely in the tin, then cut into squares. Serve individually with cream, ice cream or thick, plain yoghurt; or as they are with a cup of tea or coffee.

Oat plum breakfast cake

You might not make this delicious cake for breakfast every day, but I urge you to make it once or twice when plums are in season. It does make a deliciously shameless breakfast... The base is packed with dried fruit, honey, oats and seeds, giving it a tempting chew that's a little like a chewy flapjack. I've balanced the healthy, nutritious base with a thick smothering of whipped cream cheese, sugar, vanilla and yoghurt. I think it does the job. Keep an eye on the plums so they don't break down too much – you want them to hold a little shape. The poppy seeds are optional, but I always add a sprinkling of them at the end.

SERVES 6–8

FOR THE BASE

150g (5½oz) medium porridge oats

75g (2½oz) runny honey

25g (1oz) sunflower seeds

125g (4½oz) dried dates, destoned

75g (2½oz) prunes

FOR THE FILLING

150ml (5fl oz) double cream

1 tsp vanilla extract

40g (1½oz) icing sugar

200g (7oz) full-fat cream cheese

75g (2½oz) yoghurt

FOR THE TOPPING

½ teaspoon unsalted butter

2 teaspoons runny honey

10–12 small plums, halved and destoned

poppy seeds, for sprinkling (optional)

Cover the base of a 20cm (8in) springform tin with baking parchment, then assemble the tin, leaving some parchment to overhang around the sides. This will allow you to remove the cake easily once it's set.

To make the base, blitz all the ingredients with 2 tablespoons of water in a food processor, until crumbly and fully combined. Press the mixture into the bottom of the springform tin – it should come up to about 1cm (½in) high – and smooth it over with the back of a spoon. Place in the fridge to set while you make the filling.

In a large bowl or electric mixer, combine the filling ingredients using a whisk, making sure there are no unsightly lumps of icing sugar. Then, remove the base from the fridge and pour the mixture over. Put the tin back into the fridge for the cake to set.

Heat the butter and honey in a small frying pan over a medium heat until bubbling. Add the plums, cut-side down, and leave to fry in the sweetened butter for about 5 minutes, turning once, until softened but retaining their shape. If the plums start to fall apart, remove them from the heat. A syrup should have formed in the base of the frying pan. Set the whole lot aside and leave to cool.

To assemble the cake, remove it from the fridge and gently spoon the plums and their syrup over the top. Release the cheesecake from the springform tin, then transfer it to a serving plate. Finish with a sprinkling of poppy seeds, if you like, before serving.

Oatmeal with chicken skin & leeks

This dish contains some of my favourite ingredients: crispy, salty chicken skin; young, tender, buttery sweet leek, with its silk-on-the-teeth texture; intense, creamy and comforting pinhead oatmeal, cooked a little like risotto rice and rich like the best bread sauce; and, if you can find them, English summer truffles, with their subtle, earthy aroma. (A scant trickle of good truffle oil would be good as well.) In truth, this is a simple and a rather humble plate of food.

SERVES 2

50g (1¾oz) pinhead oatmeal

skin from 4 free-range chicken breasts

1 shallot or ½ small onion, sliced

2 garlic cloves, peeled and sliced

1 bay leaf

3 or 4 thyme sprigs

a splash of cider (optional)

300ml (10½fl oz) chicken stock (see p. 58), plus extra for loosening, if necessary

1 tablespoon grated hard cheese, such as Cheddar or Parmesan

2 knobs of butter

2 small leeks, trimmed

a few shavings of fresh truffle (optional)

salt and freshly ground black pepper

Heat the oven to 180°C/350°F/gas mark 4. Place the oatmeal in a bowl and cover with water. Set aside to soak while you crisp up the chicken skin. Line a large roasting tray with baking parchment and lay over your chicken skins, neatly and evenly spaced. Season with salt and pepper, then place in the oven for 15–20 minutes (or a bit longer if necessary), until crisp. Remove the skins to a rack to cool.

Pour 1 tablespoon of the fat from the tray into a medium heavy-based pan. Place the pan over a medium heat and add the shallot or onion, garlic, bay leaf and thyme leaves. Cook, stirring regularly, for 3–5 minutes, until the shallot is soft but not coloured. Drain the softened oatmeal through a sieve and add it to the pan. Stir well, then pour in the cider (if using) and bring to a simmer over a medium–low heat. Pour in half the stock, then allow the mixture to simmer, stirring regularly, until the stock is nearly all absorbed. Add the remaining stock and stir well. Cook for about 15–20 minutes, until you have a relatively loose porridge and the oatmeal has lost its nutty bite. Remove from the heat and stir in the cheese and 1 knob of butter, allowing them to melt into the mixture, then season well to taste and set aside.

Place the remaining butter and 100ml (3½fl oz) water in a large heavy-based pan. Lay the leeks in the pan, season well and place a lid on top. Cook for 10–15 minutes, or until tender.

To serve, warm the oatmeal through (you may need to loosen it with a little extra hot stock), then divide it equally between two plates. Place a warm leek on each plate along with some shards of crisp chicken skin and a few shavings of truffle, if using. Serve straight away.

Oat biscuits with sheep's cheese & rosemary

These little savoury oat biscuits are made with medium oatmeal and rolled porridge oats and then finished with a scattering of jumbo oats for luck. I add sheep's cheese and lots of rosemary to give them a really good flavour. A pinch or two of hot smoked paprika adds a subtle spice and a smoky edge, but that's totally optional. The oatcakes are great spread with a soft cream cheese and eaten with some wedges of apple.

MAKES 18–20

150g (5½oz) medium oatmeal

50g (1¾oz) porridge oats

75g (2½oz) hard sheep's or goat's cheese, grated

3 rosemary sprigs, leaves picked and finely chopped from 2 of them; 1 left whole

½ teaspoon fine sea salt

2 teaspoons coarsely cracked black pepper

1 or 2 pinches of hot smoked paprika (optional)

1 small handful of jumbo oats

Heat the oven to 160°C/315°F/gas mark 2–3.

Thoroughly combine the oatmeal, porridge oats, cheese, chopped rosemary leaves, salt, pepper, and paprika (if using) in a bowl. Pour 125ml (4fl oz) water over and use a wooden spoon to bring it all together to form a relatively firm, yet slightly sticky dough. Set the dough aside to rest for 10 minutes, then roll it out on a well-floured surface. Scatter over the jumbo oats and tear over the whole rosemary sprig. Roll the dough again so that the oats and rosemary stick to its surface and until the dough is about 5mm (¼in) thick.

Use a 5–6cm (2–2½in) biscuit cutter (or rim of a fine glass) to cut rounds from the dough. Place the cut rounds directly on a non-stick baking tray and bake in the oven for about 25–30 minutes, until golden.

Remove the oat biscuits to a wire rack to cool completely, before transferring to an airtight container to store. They will keep like this for up to a week.

Malted wheat loaf

I love the flavour of malted wheat flour so much. The malting process sweetens the grain and gives it a beautiful, almost caramelized flavour. You can smell its aroma when you knead, as it proves and, of course, as it bakes. It's everywhere. You can buy malted wheat flour in most supermarkets, but the quantities and the method are the same if you use only strong white.

MAKES 1 LOAF

300g (10½oz) malted wheat flour

200g (7oz) strong white bread flour, plus extra for dusting

1 teaspoon instant dried yeast

10g (¼oz) fine sea salt

sunflower oil, for oiling

Combine the flours, yeast and salt in a large mixing bowl. Add 350ml (12fl oz) water and, with one hand, mix to a rough dough. Adjust the consistency if you need to, adding a little more flour or water, until you have a soft, easily kneadable, sticky dough.

Turn out the dough onto a lightly floured work surface and knead for about 10 minutes, until smooth, stretchy and no longer sticky. Shape into a rough round. Wipe the mixing bowl clean, then oil the surface of the dough, put it back in the cleaned bowl, cover with cling film and leave to prove for 1–2 hours, or until doubled in size (the timing will depend upon the temperature in your kitchen).

Heat the oven to 220°C/425°F/gas mark 7. Deflate the dough by tipping it out of the bowl and onto the work surface. Press it into a rudimentary rectangle shape, with a short end nearest your body. Fold the nearest third into the middle, then the third furthest from you over the top of this. Seal the loaf at its seams. Give it a quarter turn, stretch it out and repeat, third over third. Using the palms of your hands roll the dough into a cylindrical baton about 25cm (10in) in length, tapering a little at the ends. Set the baton on a well-floured surface. Sprinkle with flour and leave to rise for a further 20–25 minutes.

Heat a baking sheet in the oven until hot. Remove the tray from the oven, then without knocking the air out of the risen dough, lift it very carefully off the work surface and onto the hot tray. Use a serrated knife to slash a cut 2cm (¾in) deep down the length of the baton. This will help the dough spring up in the oven. Bake for 25–30 minutes, then lower the oven temperature to 180°C/350°F/gas mark 4 and bake for a further 20 minutes until a dark, golden crust has formed and the loaf sounds hollow when tapped. Remove to a rack to cool.

Focaccia

Focaccia is a medium for all sorts of other wonderful ingredients. Here, I use sweet onions, chunky bacon and a handful of fresh sage and rosemary – but the possibilities are endless. Beetroot and blue cheese is a favourite, as is apple, cheddar and hazelnut, or black pudding and ripe tomatoes, strewn with plenty of fresh thyme and trickled with olive oil. Two or three trays of this bacon-and-onion focaccia passed around at a gathering always go down well. With a few salads and drinks alongside, it's a bread that becomes a complete meal.

MAKES 1 LOAF

500g (1lb 2oz) strong white bread flour, plus extra for dusting

10g (¼oz) fine sea salt

1 teaspoon instant dried yeast

50ml (1½fl oz) extra-virgin olive oil, plus extra for oiling and drizzling

FOR THE TOPPING

250g (9oz) large bacon lardons

1 large onion, thickly sliced

1 large bunch of mixed herbs, such as sage leaves, thyme leaves, and torn rosemary sprigs

salt and freshly ground black pepper

Place the flour, fine sea salt and yeast in a large bowl, add the oil and 400ml (14fl oz) water and combine to a fairly wet dough. Turn out the dough onto a lightly floured surface and knead it for about 10 minutes, until it is soft and smooth. (Use a mixer with a dough hook for this part, if you have one.)

Form the dough into a rough round and drop it into a lightly oiled bowl, cover with a clean tea towel or cling film and leave to prove in a warm place for 1½−2 hours, or until doubled in size.

Meanwhile, heat a dash of oil in a large frying pan over a medium heat. Add the bacon lardons and fry for 3−4 minutes, or until rendering a little fat. Scatter in the onion, season, toss well and cook for a further 10−12 minutes, or until the onion is beginning to soften. Remove the pan from the heat and allow to cool.

When the dough is ready, heat the oven to 200°C/400°F/gas mark 6. Lightly grease a 22 x 30cm (8½ x 12in) baking tray, and dust it with a little flour (or polenta). Turn out the dough onto the greased tray, and press it outward lightly with your fingertips so that it covers the tray. Scatter over the cooked lardon and onion mixture in an even layer. Spike and spear the whole dough with the herbs, as roughly as you care. Press everything deep into the dough with your fingers. Cover the tray and leave to rise for a further 35−45 minutes. Uncover the tray and carefully prod the bacon and onions back down into the risen dough. Drizzle generously with olive oil and place the focaccia on the middle shelf of the oven for 35−40 minutes, until cooked through and golden. Remove the focaccia from the oven, drizzle with a little more olive oil and sprinkle over some salt. Eat warm.

Pasta pappardelle

There's something very satisfying about making your own pasta. I think it's the fact that it's such a common commodity, the idea of actually making it seems a little alien to most (the same is true of bread-making). Yet making pasta is so simple and uses the most basic of ingredients: wheat flour and fresh eggs. This recipe makes a silky, tender pasta that you can cut into large lasagne sheets, lengths of slender tagliatelle, or (my favourite) bold-ribboned pappardelle.

SERVES 4

400g (14oz) type oo (double zero) flour, plus extra for dusting

good pinch of fine sea salt

4 eggs

Place the flour in a large bowl and add the salt. Make a well in the centre and crack in the eggs. Use a fork to whisk the eggs and slowly start to incorporate the flour, a little at a time. When you have a soft dough, tip it out, along with any loose flour, onto a clean surface. Work the dough, stretching and folding it across your work surface for 8–10 minutes, until it is smooth and silky. Wrap the dough in clingfilm and rest it in the fridge for 30–40 minutes.

Divide the dough in half and work each into a flattish rectangle in your hands. You can roll out the pasta using a large rolling pin (it's hard work, but you'll get there – go as thin as you can), but it's easier using a pasta machine. Take one rectangle and pass it through the machine on its thickest setting a couple of times. Fold the dough into three, as if folding a letter, and, still on the thickest setting, pass it through twice more (this gives the dough structure).

Now, run the dough half through all the settings on the machine, from its thickest to its thinnest. Dust both sides of the pasta lightly with flour each time you roll. When you've got down to the thinnest setting, cut the pasta into long ribbons to make the pappardelle. I hang the lengths over the back of a chair while I roll and cut the remaining dough, as before. The pasta will dry quite quickly so if you don't intend to cook it straight away, layer it up between sheets of cling film and keep it covered in the fridge. Repeat the rolling and cutting process with the other dough half.

Cook the pasta in plenty of salted boiling water for 3–6 minutes, until cooked to your liking (the timing will vary according to the thickness and shape of the pasta, so be on hand to test it). Serve it simply stirred through some melted butter with sage leaves and parmesan, or with your favourite sauce (try the rabbit sauce on p. 218).

Barley, squash & mushrooms with herb & crème fraîche dressing

This is an earthy, nutty and substantial salad, full of good textures and early autumn flavours. Barley is curious in that it never really overcooks in the way rice can. It retains its charming, slightly toothsome bite, which is just perfect with the buttery, sweet roasted squash and tender mushrooms. The dressing is full of fresh dill, a herb with a reassuring, familiar flavour that I like very much, particularly with mushrooms and grains.

SERVES 4–6

250g (9oz) pearl barley

4 tablespoons extra-virgin olive oil

zest and juice of 1 lemon

1 large butternut or crown prince squash

1 small bunch of sage, leaves picked

6–8 rosemary sprigs

1 small garlic bulb, cloves separated, skin on

4 or 5 large portobello mushrooms or similar (about 300–400g/ 10½–14oz)

2 teaspoons sugar

2 teaspoons English or Dijon mustard

1 tablespoon cider vinegar

2–3 tablespoons crème fraîche

1 good bunch of dill fronds, finely chopped, plus extra for serving

1 bunch of flat-leaf parsley, leaves picked

salt and freshly ground black pepper

Heat the oven to 180°C/350°F/gas mark 4. Place the pearl barley in a medium pan, cover with water, and place on a medium heat. Simmer gently for 25–30 minutes, until the barley is tender with a slightly nutty bite. Drain and immediately dress with half the olive oil, the lemon zest and juice and a little salt. Set aside to cool.

Place the squash on a board and cut it in half lengthways. Scoop out the seeds, then cut each half into 5 or 6 wedges and place them in a large roasting tray along with the sage leaves and rosemary sprigs, garlic cloves, the remaining olive oil and a generous seasoning of salt and black pepper. Cover the roasting tray with foil and place in the oven for 30–40 minutes, until soft. Meanwhile, slice the mushrooms into 3–4cm (1¼–1½in) slices.

Take the roasting tray out of the oven, remove the foil and scatter the sliced mushrooms over and around it. Turn everything together carefully to avoid breaking up the squash, then return it, uncovered, to the oven and cook for a further 20 minutes, until the mushrooms are cooked and the squash has taken on some colour. Remove from the oven and allow to cool.

To make the dressing, thoroughly combine the sugar, mustard and vinegar in a small bowl. Stir in the crème fraîche and the chopped dill, and season with salt and pepper, to taste.

To serve, tumble the squash, mushrooms, herbs, garlic and all the juices in the roasting tray together with the barley. Scatter over the parsley leaves, spoon over the dressing, tumble again, then finish with a scattering of dill. Take to the table straight away.

Stuffed squash with fennel & barley

Whenever I make these little stuffed squash, I'm reminded of being with my friend Pip, who is sadly not around any more. Preparing and cooking mixed pumpkins and squash, just like I do here, was the last thing we did together, for a book we were working on at the time. I remember it as if it were yesterday. This variation is sweet from the squash and roasted fennel, and full of character from the barley. I think Pip would definitely approve.

SERVES 2

2 small onion squash (about 800g/1lb 12oz each)

2 fennel bulbs

2 tablespoons extra-virgin olive oil

1 handful of fennel tops, if available

125g (4½oz) pearl barley

100g (3½oz) Cheddar cheese, grated

25g (1oz) butter

1 garlic clove, peeled and grated

salt and freshly ground black pepper

Heat the oven to 180°C/350°F/gas mark 4. Use a sharp, heavy knife to cut the base off each squash, so that they sit upright. Cut off the tops in one, clean round, about 3cm (1¼in) or so below the stalk, and set aside. Use a metal spoon to scoop out the seeds and the fibrous matter, to leave a fairly neat hollow.

Trim the fennel, and remove the tougher outer leaf if you need to. Cut the bulbs in half, then cut each half into 3 or 4 wedges.

Place the squash in a large roasting tray. Scatter the fennel wedges around them and try to squeeze in the squash tops, too. Drizzle the olive oil all over, including inside the squash. Season with salt and pepper and scatter over a few fennel tops, if you have them. Place the tray in the oven and cook for 45–60 minutes, or until both the squash and the fennel are nice and tender. If the fennel starts to take on too much colour, cover the tray with tin foil.

Meanwhile, place the barley in a medium pan and cover it with water. Place on a medium heat and simmer gently for 25–30 minutes, until the barley is soft but still retains some bite. Drain well and place in a large bowl. When the fennel and squash are cooked, remove them from the oven and add the roasted fennel to the barley, then add the cheese, butter, grated garlic and plenty of salt and pepper to taste. Tumble everything together and spoon the barley mixture equally into the two roasted squash. Return the tray to the oven for 8–10 minutes to heat through, then serve straight away with their lids, and some soured cream and a green salad.

Butter-roasted barley flakes & leeks

Crisp, buttery barley flakes lift this simple variation on leeks vinaigrette to a completely new, deeply textured level. Good bread is all it really needs to make a fine lunch for two or a lighter starter for four. It also makes a fitting accompaniment to warm lemony roast chicken or a piece of freshly grilled fish.

SERVES 2 AS A LUNCH OR 4 AS A STARTER

2 teaspoons Dijon mustard

1 teaspoon runny honey

2 tablespoons extra-virgin olive oil

2 knobs of butter

50g (1¾oz) rolled barley flakes

1 small garlic clove, bashed

4 small leeks, trimmed

5 or 6 thyme sprigs

1 bay leaf

salt and freshly ground black pepper

First, make the dressing. Combine the mustard, honey and olive oil in a small bowl with a little salt and pepper, and set aside.

Melt half the butter in a large heavy-based frying pan over a medium heat, until it's gently bubbling. Add the barley flakes along with plenty of salt and pepper. Stir to coat the barley in the butter, add the garlic, then cook, shaking and stirring the pan regularly to ensure the flakes toast evenly. It should take about 6–8 minutes to crisp the flakes and bring out their fragrant aroma.

Use a slotted spoon or spatula to remove the barley from the hot butter to a plate lined with kitchen paper.

Cut away most of the of the darker green tops of the leeks (you can save them for making stock). Cut the remaining parts of the leeks into 2.5cm (1in) rounds on a slight angle. Give them a wash in plenty of water, but be careful not to break up the rounds too much.

Drain the leeks and place them in a shallow pan. Add the remaining butter, thyme sprigs and bay leaf and half a glass of water, and season well with salt and pepper. Place the lid on the pan and set it over a medium heat. Bring the contents of the pan up to a very gentle simmer, then cook, covered, for 6–8 minutes, or until the leeks are tender. Drain the leeks in a colander and allow them to cool a little. Arrange the cooled leeks over a large serving platter, scatter over the toasted rolled barley and drizzle over the dressing. Serve straight away.

Barbecued corn & red onions with corn purée

Corn is a different beast when it's barbecued: the hot coals blister the kernels, rendering them charred and sugary-sweet, and accentuate everything that's good – even the yellow gets yellower. Here, I've served barbecued corn alongside more corn – a purée of kernels cut from the cob that couldn't look more different from their blackened counterparts. The purée is absolutely delicious: onions softened in butter and olive oil give it body, and it's loosened by a good stock. As a little addition, I colour red onions over the barbecue at the same time as I cook the corn-on-the-cobs. They burn here and there, bringing a bitter vibe to the sweet party.

SERVES 4

1 large knob of butter

1 tablespoon extra-virgin olive oil, plus extra for grilling

1 onion, thinly sliced

2 thyme sprigs, leaves stripped

6 corn-on-the-cobs, papery husks stripped

about 400ml (14fl oz) vegetable stock or chicken stock (see p. 58)

2 red onions, quartered, skin on and root intact

salt and freshly ground black pepper

Heat the butter and olive oil in a medium heavy-based pan over a low heat, until it starts to bubble. Then, add the sliced onion, the thyme leaves and a little salt and pepper. Turn down the heat to low and cook gently, stirring regularly, for about 15 minutes, until the onion is soft. Using a sharp knife, remove the kernels from two of the corn cobs. Add these to the onions, then add the stock.

Simmer the contents of the pan for 25 minutes, until the stock has reduced by about half and the corn is tender. Tip the softened corn into a jug and use a stick blender to purée until smooth. Alternatively, place in a food processor or blender and blitz. Taste and adjust the seasoning if necessary.

Light your barbecue, or place a griddle pan over a medium heat. The onions and corn need to cook through, so you don't want the heat too hot – your barbecue is ready when you can hold your hand over the grilling rack for only 1–2 seconds.

Place the quartered red onions on a baking tray with the remaining corn cobs, season with salt and pepper and drizzle over a little olive oil. Place the corns and the onions on the barbecue grill bars or on your griddle. Cook, turning regularly, for 25–30 minutes or until the corn and the onions are tender and blistered. Remove to a plate and set aside.

To serve, spoon a little corn purée onto each plate, then add a piece of barbecued corn and a few onion wedges. Serve straight away with hunks of good bread.

Polenta with roast ham & parsley

If you haven't had polenta before, you must try this recipe. Traditionally, polenta is served 'wet' or 'soft', which means it comes to the table like a porridge or a thick purée. Alternatively, you can serve it 'set' – when loose polenta is cooled and set in the fridge, then cut into wedges and fried. This recipe, though, sticks with tradition. A delicious wet polenta made with well-flavoured ham stock, it is served with the ham itself. To me, the entire dish makes complete and utter sense from the first mouthful to the last. It's perfectly simple and so, so comforting. Make this when you need a massive hug in a bowl.

SERVES 4

1 ham hock (about 1–1.5kg/2lb 4oz–3lb 5oz)

1 onion, halved

1 carrot

1 small garlic bulb, halved around its circumference

1 bunch of parsley, leaves picked and chopped, stalks reserved

4 thyme sprigs

4 bay leaves

1 teaspoon peppercorns

2 tablespoons soft brown sugar

2 tablespoons Dijon mustard

1 bunch of sage, leaves picked

150g (5½oz) fine polenta

50g (1¾oz) hard sheep's cheese or Cheddar, grated

1 knob of butter

salt and freshly ground black pepper

Rinse the ham hock in water, then place it in a large pan and add water to cover. Add the onion halves, whole carrot, garlic halves, parsley stalks, thyme sprigs, bay leaves and peppercorns, and place the pan on a medium–high heat. As the contents of the pan come up to the boil, turn down the heat to a simmer and skim away any froth that rises to the surface. Simmer, uncovered, for 3 hours, or until the meat is tender and comes away from the bone with ease.

Heat the oven to 180°C/350°F/gas mark 4. Lift the hock into a small roasting tray, reserving the stock. When the meat is cool enough to handle, peel away the soft skin and place it underneath the meat. Combine the sugar and mustard, then spoon the mixture over the meat. Scatter over the sage leaves, and roast in the oven for 25–30 minutes, until bubbling and caramelized. Remove from the oven and keep warm.

Meanwhile, pass the ham stock through a fine sieve into a bowl and set aside. Use the back of a spoon to push through as much flavour from the vegetables as possible. Bring 750–800ml (26fl oz–28fl oz) of the stock up to a gentle simmer in a large, heavy-based pan. Pour in the polenta in a slow, steady stream, stirring well as you add it. It will thicken quite quickly, but will need gentle simmering for 6–8 minutes, until the grain is cooked properly. If it becomes too thick, add a dash more stock. Stir in the cheese, butter and chopped parsley, and season, if necessary.

Divide the polenta between four plates. Shred, tear and cut off chunks of ham and pile them onto the polenta. Spoon over any roasting juices and bring to the table straight away.

Sweetcorn & smoked haddock soup with soft-boiled eggs & coriander

I once ate a smoked fish soup in Connemara on the west coast of Ireland. You could hear the wild Atlantic Sea from where I sat, in a small pub off the beach. The flavour and simplicity of the soup remain with me, even though it was many years ago. It was all burnt oak and cream and texture and warmth. There was sweetcorn, and generous chunks of locally smoked fish – and lots of spinach. Although I have never been able to recreate it, this smoked fish soup is simple, inspired by that Connemara lunch. Be really big-hearted with the corn, as it brings a sweetness that works so well with the salty, smoky fish. If you like coriander as much as I do, add it freshly chopped by the handful, and take this soup in a new direction.

SERVES 4

4 eggs, at room temperature

1 knob of butter

1 tablespoon extra-virgin olive oil

1 large leek, trimmed and thinly sliced

2 garlic cloves, peeled and sliced

1 large or 2 small corn-on-the-cobs

400ml (14fl oz) vegetable or fish stock

150ml (5fl oz) double cream

200g (7oz) naturally smoked haddock or pollack, skinned, boned and cut into slices

1 large bunch of coriander, roughly chopped (reserve a few whole leaves for serving)

salt and freshly ground black pepper

Bring a small pan of water to the boil. Add the eggs and boil for 6½ minutes so that the yolk will be soft, but not runny. Remove the pan from the heat, drain away the hot water and cover the eggs with cold water to stop them cooking further. Set aside.

Melt the butter with the oil in a heavy-based pan over a medium heat. When it's bubbling, add the leek and garlic. Fry gently for 10–12 minutes, until the leek and garlic are soft but not coloured. Cut the corn kernels from the cob (or cobs), then add the kernels to the pan along with the stock. Bring up to a simmer and cook for a further 10–12 minutes. Add the cream and bring the contents of the pan back up to a simmer. Then, add the fish and the chopped coriander and simmer for 2–3 minutes more, until the fish is lightly cooked. Then, remove the pan from the heat, taste and adjust the seasoning, if necessary.

Peel the eggs and halve them, then place them, cut side up on the surface of the soup, allowing them 1–2 minutes to heat through.

Ladle the soup into four bowls, making sure that everyone gets two egg halves. Finish with a scattering of fresh coriander leaves and serve straight away.

woodland

woodland | Lush are the woods. We stand in your simplicity, your architecture.
You are ancient, but as fleeting as water or darkness or nothing. Deep, life, sky when you're dead, then the emerald and the red. Flanked by the expanse and the change, remain, as timber bones, the mulch and a million tones. Dank and soft, a safe home, unowned, we are lost in the gnarl of your limbs. Breathing, you are heaving, a harvest for me and for them. Invisibly sown, the strength of root, the fragility of shoots, the feasts, the fires and the fruits.

mushrooms

squirrel

cobnuts

blackberries

crab apples

Ceps with artichoke & chives

I'm not going to lie, this has to be one of my favourite plates of food ever. I love its pastoral elegance – it feels and tastes like you've stolen the soul from an autumn woodland. That feeling (accentuated perhaps by how many ciders you've drunk), is a testament to good ingredients and simple cooking. If you can't find ceps or porcini mushrooms locally during the autumn months, then, of course, you can buy them online from a variety of wild- and foraged-food specialists. There are alternatives: firm, cultivated chestnut mushrooms would work really well, too.

SERVES 2

350g (12oz; about 6–8) Jerusalem artichokes, peeled, skins reserved

2 garlic cloves, bashed but skin on

4 thyme sprigs

3 tablespoons extra-virgin olive oil

1 knob of butter

sunflower oil, for deep frying

2 large cep mushrooms, cut into 1cm (½in) slices

1 small bunch of chives, finely chopped

salt and freshly ground black pepper

Heat the oven to 180°C/350°F/gas mark 4. Cut the peeled artichokes into 3cm (1¼in) cubes. Place the cubes into a roasting tray, with the garlic cloves, thyme sprigs and 2 tablespoons of olive oil. Season all over with salt and pepper, then place in the oven. Roast, stirring once or twice, for about 1 hour, or until the artichoke cubes are tender and caramelized. Squeeze the softened garlic flesh from its skin and place it in a blender with the roasted artichoke, the butter and just enough water to loosen, then blitz to a smooth, spoonable purée. Check the seasoning and keep warm.

Wash the reserved artichoke skins, drain and pat dry (they need to be completely dry for frying). Heat 2–3cm (¾–1¼in) of sunflower oil in a medium saucepan over a medium heat. When it's hot enough for frying (170°C/325°F on a cooking thermometer; or when a cube of bread sizzles and crisps quickly), fry the skins in batches for about 1–1½ minutes each, until crisp and golden. Don't let them get too dark or they will taste bitter. Drain each batch on kitchen paper, then season with salt and set aside.

Heat the remaining olive oil in a large frying pan over a medium–high heat until hot. Season the mushroom slices with salt and pepper and place them in the pan. Fry the slices for 2–3 minutes on each side, until they have taken on some colour. Remove the pan from the heat and stir through half the chopped chives.

Divide the artichoke purée between two plates. Arrange the fried mushrooms around this, then scatter over the crispy artichoke skin peelings and the remaining chives. Serve straight away.

Puffball with bacon, parsley & garlic

In late summer and early autumn, keep your eyes open for giant puffballs, best picked when young and firm, and no bigger than 25cm (10in) or so in diameter. A puffball of this size will feed at least four people, so should you stumble across a few it's unlikely you'll need to pick them all. They're not difficult to spot – they stand out like bright white footballs amid the green of the grass. I've always been really fond of this unusual fungus. As children we used to jump on the older, wrinkled ones, and they would explode in a magical puff of spores. Good times. For cooking, I treat them simply, peeling away the thin skin, cutting them into thick slices, then frying them in butter. Sometimes, I dip the rounds in beaten egg and porridge oats to give a wonderful, crisp coating. Here, I'm cooking the puffball in the same way I would a steak – on a griddle pan, with good bacon, and some garlic and parsley – the perfect forager's breakfast.

SERVES 2

2 large, thick slices of puffball

1 tablespoon extra-virgin olive oil

4 thick rashers streaky bacon

2–4 garlic cloves, bashed

3 or 4 thyme sprigs

1 knob of butter

1 small bunch of flat-leaf parsley, leaves picked and chopped

salt and freshly ground black pepper

Heat a large heavy-based, ridged griddle pan over a high heat. While it's getting hot, peel or cut the outer skin from the puffball slices – the skin is very thin, but can be a little tough to eat. Brush the puffball slices with the olive oil and season well with salt and pepper.

When the griddle pan is nice and hot, place the prepared puffball slices in the pan. Add the bacon, the bashed garlic cloves and the thyme sprigs, and griddle for 3–4 minutes, until the undersides of the puffball slices have taken on some charring from the ridges of the grill pan. Flip the slices of puffball, and cook for a further 3–4 minutes to char the other sides. Turn the bacon 3 or 4 times throughout the cooking, until it is cooked through and nicely crisped.

Take the pan off the heat and add the butter and chopped parsley. Turn the bacon and puffball through the butter as it melts. Divide the puffball and bacon slices equally between two plates and serve straight away.

Hedgehog mushrooms on toast

My friend Johan has shown me some really good spots to gather this well-textured, yet delicate wild mushroom. It seems to grow well on the soft, earthy floor of shaded evergreen woodlands and on the high, tree-lined banks you so often see in Devon. Hedgehog mushrooms are almost impossible to mistake, being light leather in colour and the only common wild mushroom with spines instead of gills.

SERVES 2

about 250–300g (9–10½oz) hedgehog mushrooms (enough to fill a small basket)

2 slices of sourdough, or other good-quality bread

1 generous knob of butter, plus extra for the toast

1 tablespoon extra-virgin olive oil

1 garlic clove, peeled and thinly sliced

1 small bunch flat leaf-parsley, leaves picked and chopped

salt and freshly ground black pepper

Trim the earthy base away from the mushrooms and brush off any grit, soil or little leaves – it's best not to wash the mushrooms unless you really have to. Slice, toast and butter the sourdough. Heat the oil in a large, heavy-based frying pan over a high heat. When it's hot, throw in the hedgehogs and season with salt and pepper. These mushrooms have quite a high water content, so cook them, tossing occasionally, for 3–4 minutes until the water in them has evaporated. Now clear a small space in the pan into which you can place the large knob of butter. When the butter is bubbling, add the sliced garlic and cook for 1 minute in the space in the pan, to soften a little, before tossing everything together.

Add the chopped parsley leaves to the pan and stir everything through to combine. Pile the mushrooms on the toast, dividing them equally between the two slices, and serve straight away.

Roast squirrel with squash, sage & hazelnuts

The following three recipes will work really well with rabbit, pheasant or even chicken, but I'm suggesting using squirrel as a first port of call. It's relatively easy to get hold of these days (try wildmeat.co.uk) and it is, without question, one of the most sustainable meats we could ever hope to eat. This is such a simple and delicious way to cook squirrel. I'd recommend it to anyone, especially if you like getting hands-on with your food. This is the sort of dish I'd share with a friend, straight from the roasting tin, all salty fingers and smiles, with a good bottle of red wine. The meat is surprisingly tender and responds so well to the high heat of the oven. The pumpkin, sage and nuts are perfect with the squirrel, making this an ultimate autumn dish... albeit in a curious, Beatrix Potter kind of way.

SERVES 2 AS A STARTER

2 thick slices of butternut squash (about 250g/9oz)

1 oven-ready squirrel (about 250g/9oz, jointed on the bone), or 4 pheasant or 2 chicken thighs on the bone, or 1 small rabbit (jointed)

1 garlic bulb, halved around its circumference

1 handful of sage leaves

2 bay leaves

2 tablespoons whole hazelnuts

2 tablespoons extra-virgin olive oil

salt and freshly ground black pepper

Heat the oven to 190°C/375°F/gas mark 5. Place the squash slices in a medium roasting tray and arrange the squirrel (or pheasant, chicken or rabbit) pieces around it. Nestle in the two halves of the garlic bulb, then sage leaves and bay leaves, and then scatter over the hazelnuts. Drizzle over the olive oil and season everything well with salt and pepper.

Place the tray in the oven and roast for 45–60 minutes, turning the squirrel pieces once during this time, until the squash is cooked and the squirrel is tender. Remove the tray from the oven and allow the meat to rest for 4–5 minutes.

Divide the squirrel meat and squash evenly between two plates, along with a few cloves of the tender, roasted garlic. Serve straight away. (Or bring the roasting tin to the table and eat it straight from the tin.)

Crispy squirrel with cauliflower & capers

I cook this delicate meat with onions, carrots, celery and herbs, very gently, until it's fork-tender and the meat is falling away from the bone. Then I fry it hard, in shards, with garlic, rosemary and pungent salty capers so that it crisps and caramelizes around the edges – a seriously wicked treatment for this hugely underrated wild meat.

SERVES 4

1 oven-ready squirrel (about 250g/9oz, jointed on the bone), or 4 pheasant or 2 chicken thighs on the bone, or 1 small rabbit (jointed)

2 onions

1 carrot, peeled and roughly chopped

1 celery stick, roughly chopped

2 bay leaves

2 thyme sprigs

1 small knob of butter

2 tablespoons extra-virgin olive oil, plus extra for drizzling

½ head of cauliflower (about 400g/14oz), outer leaves removed

2 rosemary sprigs

3–4 teaspoons small capers

1 garlic clove, peeled and very thinly sliced

salt and freshly ground black pepper

4 slices of good-quality rustic bread, toasted, to serve

Place the squirrel (or pheasant, chicken or rabbit) into a small– medium pan so that the pieces of meat fit snugly in a single layer. Roughly chop 1 onion and add it to the pan with the carrot, celery, bay leaves and thyme sprigs. Cover with water. Place the pan on a high heat and bring to a simmer. Turn down the heat to low and cook, uncovered, for 1½–2 hours, skimming the cooking liquor occasionally, until the squirrel meat is falling off the bone. Once the meat is ready, strain the cooking liquid into a bowl and reserve. Discard the vegetables and set the squirrel meat aside to cool.

Finely chop the remaining onion. Melt the butter with half the oil in a medium pan over a medium heat. When it's bubbling, add the onion. Cook gently for 4–5 minutes, until the onion is soft but not coloured. Meanwhile, roughly slice the cauliflower, first trimming and discarding any rough stem. When the onions are softened, add the cauliflower to the pan. Pour over 150ml (5fl oz) of the reserved cooking liquid and place a lid on the pan. Cook for 4–5 minutes, or until the cauliflower is just tender. Transfer to a blender, and blitz to a smooth, velvety purée. Season, then keep warm.

Flake the squirrel meat off the bone, trying to keep it in larger chunks and shards. Heat the remaining tablespoon of oil in a medium frying pan over a high heat, and add the squirrel, chicken or game meat. Fry for 3–4 minutes, until the pieces are starting to crisp around the edges. Tear over the rosemary, add the capers and garlic, stir, and season. Fry for 3–4 minutes, tossing regularly, until the meat is caramelized, then remove from the heat.

Place one slice of toast on each plate, drizzle over some olive oil and spoon the puréed cauliflower over each slice. Top with the squirrel mixture and serve straight away.

Squirrel, rosemary & potato rösti

I like this rösti because it's so very different, which probably has something to do with the squirrel — although lamb, pheasant or rabbit would be good contenders for a substitute. I've also done a very similar — and equally delicious — thing with wild oysters on a blustery beach on the isle of Islay in Scotland, but that's another story. Use a good non-stick pan for cooking this all-in-one supper dish — it will make everything easier.

SERVES 2

1 oven-ready squirrel (about 250g/9oz, jointed on the bone), or 4 pheasant or 2 chicken thighs on the bone, or 1 small rabbit (jointed)

2 potatoes (about 400g/14oz) — choose a white, floury variety, such as Wilja, King Edward or Maris Piper, peeled and coarsely grated

2 rosemary sprigs

2 tablespoons extra-virgin olive oil

salt and freshly ground black pepper

fried egg, to serve (optional)

green salad, to serve (optional)

Use a sharp knife to take the meat off the bone — the largest proportion of which is on the hind legs of the squirrel, but there's also meat to remove on the saddle and front legs. Place the meat on a board and chop it into small, 3–5mm (⅛–¼in) pieces, so that you make a chunky mince. (If using pheasant breasts, or other alternative, chop into small pieces.) Set aside.

Squeeze out as much starchy liquid from the grated potato as possible — pick up small amounts and squeeze it really hard in your hands, letting the liquid run off. Once you've squeezed all the potato, place it in a bowl and add the squirrel meat. Crudely tear the rosemary sprigs into the bowl, season well with salt and pepper and use your hands to tumble everything together.

Heat the olive oil in a medium non-stick frying pan over a medium–high heat. Scatter in the potato-and-squirrel mixture, creating an even layer in the pan. Use the back of a spatula to press it down so the top is relatively smooth and you have an even shape.

Once you've got a nice, flat layer and you can hear it sizzling away, turn the heat right down to low. Cook the rösti for 12–15 minutes, occasionally pressing it down with a spatula, until the underside has taken on some colour (carefully free it with the spatula to take a look). When it has, carefully flip over the rösti in one piece. If you're having trouble, invert it out of the pan onto a plate, then slide it from the plate back into the pan.

Cook the other side for 12–15 minutes, until it's crispy and browned, then invert the rösti onto a plate. Serve it topped with a fried egg and/or a sharply dressed green salad.

Cobnut, prune & chocolate tart

This nutty, chocolatey pudding is a fine way to round off a good lunch or weekend supper. If you can't find fresh cobnuts you can use hazelnuts instead.

SERVES 10—12

100g (3½oz) juicy stoned prunes, halved if large

50g (1¾oz) dark chocolate drops, at least 70 per cent cocoa solids

85g (3oz) shelled cobnuts or hazelnuts, roughly chopped

oats, for sprinkling

3 tablespoons apple brandy

FOR THE PASTRY

90g (3¼oz) icing sugar

340g (11¾oz) plain flour

170g (5¾oz) butter, cubed and chilled, plus extra for greasing

1 egg

2 tablespoons iced water

FOR THE BUTTERSCOTCH FILLING

50g (1¾oz) golden caster sugar

1 small knob of butter

125ml (4fl oz) double cream

pinch of fine sea salt

FOR THE FRANGIPANE

75g (2½oz) unsalted butter

75g (2½oz) golden caster sugar

2 eggs, beaten

75g (2½oz) ground hazelnuts

First, make the pastry. Combine the icing sugar and plain flour in a medium bowl. Rub in the chilled butter cubes until the mixture resembles fine breadcrumbs (you can also do this in a food processor). Add in the egg and iced water, and stir through to combine. Tip out the dough and bring it together with your hands, kneading lightly to achieve a smooth finish. Wrap the pastry tightly in cling film and place it in the fridge to rest for at least 30 minutes.

Heat the oven to 180°C/350°F/gas mark 4. On a lightly floured surface, roll out the pastry until it is about 2mm (¹⁄₁₆in) thick. Grease and flour a 25cm (10in) loose-bottomed tart tin, then lay over the pastry, tucking it into the corners and leaving an overhang. Line the pastry case with baking parchment and baking beans. Blind bake the tart case for 25 minutes, then remove the baking beans, trim the overhang, and return to the oven for 10 minutes, or until the base is just starting to colour. Remove and set aside.

To make the butterscotch, place the sugar in a small heavy-based pan. Add 1 tablespoon of water and place the pan on a medium heat. Bring the sugar to a simmer, agitating the pan to help all the sugar dissolve and caramelize. When you have a nutty, golden colour, remove from the heat and, stirring continuously, add the butter followed by the cream. Mix for 1—2 minutes, until you have a smooth, even sauce. Season with a pinch of salt and allow to cool.

For the frangipane, cream the butter and sugar until light and fluffy. Add the eggs and hazelnuts, and mix until combined.

Spread the butterscotch over the base of the tart case, then spoon over the frangipane. Scatter over the prunes, chocolate drops and chopped cobnuts and finish with a sprinkling of oats. Bake in the oven for 12—15 minutes, or until just set. Remove the tart from the oven and allow to cool for 15—20 minutes before serving with cream or ice cream.

Cobnut & celeriac soup with kale, parsley & olive oil

Cobnuts bring an unexpected dimension to this gorgeous soup. They're fresh and fleshy and their flavour, being delicate and sweet, works beautifully with robust kale and earthy celeriac. If you're making your own stock, make sure it's really tasty before you add it to the rest of the soup ingredients. That way you're guaranteed the most amazing results. I like to slip in some toasted sourdough or other good country-style bread to the bowls before bringing to the table.

SERVES 4

4 tablespoons extra-virgin olive oil, plus extra for drizzling

400g (14oz) celeriac, peeled and cut into 2cm (¾in) cubes

1 onion, finely diced

3 or 4 thyme sprigs

50g (1¾oz) shelled cobnuts, roughly chopped

2 garlic cloves, peeled and grated, plus an extra clove, halved, for rubbing

4–6 sage leaves, torn

1 litre (35fl oz) good-quality, chicken (see p. 58) or vegetable stock

1 small bunch Tuscan or curly kale (about 75g/2½oz), tough stem removed, leaves roughly chopped

1 bunch flat-leaf parsley, finely chopped

salt and freshly ground black pepper

toasted or chargrilled bread, for serving

Heat the olive oil in a large heavy-based pan over a medium heat. Add the celeriac, diced onion and thyme sprigs. Cook, stirring regularly, for 5–6 minutes, until the onion is soft but not coloured, then season the celeriac with salt and pepper. Scatter over the chopped nuts, the grated garlic, and the torn sage leaves and stir well. Cook for 1–2 minutes more, then add the stock and bring the contents of the pan up to a simmer.

Cook gently for 8–10 minutes until the celeriac is tender, then add the chopped kale and return to a simmer. Cook for a further 10 minutes, until the kale is tender, then remove the soup from the heat. Add the chopped parsley to the pan, then season well with salt and pepper.

Ladle the soup into bowls and serve with some toasted or chargrilled bread rubbed with a halved garlic clove and sprinkled with flaky salt, then drizzled with your best olive oil.

Cobnut, yoghurt & honeycomb cake

This unusual cake is made with natural yoghurt and only the smallest amount of flour. It's got a subtle acidity and can be smooth and delicate. In the autumn, though, nuts and crunchy honeycomb bring texture, contrast and earthy sweetness. You can make the same cake with hazelnuts rather than cobnuts and you can leave out the honeycomb if you find it too sweet.

SERVES 8

FOR THE HONEYCOMB
a little sunflower oil, for brushing

75g (2½oz) golden caster sugar

small pinch of fine sea salt

1 teaspoon bicarbonate of soda

FOR THE CAKE
butter, for greasing

4 eggs, separated

85g (3oz) golden caster sugar

500ml (17fl oz) plain natural yoghurt

zest of ½ orange

35g (1¼oz) plain flour

100g (3½oz) cobnuts, shelled and lightly broken

First, make the honeycomb (it's pretty easy). Lay out a non-stick silicone mat, or a piece of lightly oiled baking parchment over a baking sheet. Melt the sugar with the pinch of salt in a small, heavy-based non-stick pan over a medium heat, for about 6–8 minutes, until it is just melted but still very light in colour. You can encourage the sugar to melt by gently agitating the pan every so often. Be very careful that the sugar doesn't burn, which would give it a bitter flavour.

As soon as the sugar is ready, add the bicarbonate of soda to the pan in a single sprinkling motion and work it in quickly with a wooden spoon. If all goes to plan, the sugar will froth and pillow. Stir it quickly and carefully for 2–3 seconds, then pour it out over the silicone mat or oiled baking parchment. Leave the honeycomb undisturbed for 15–20 minutes, until it has cooled and firmed up.

Heat the oven to 150°C/300°F/gas mark 2. Lightly grease a 20cm (8in) cake tin. Place the egg yolks in a food mixer fitted with a whisk attachment. Add two-thirds of the sugar and whisk for 5 minutes, until thick and pale. Gently fold in the yoghurt, then the orange zest, then the flour.

In a separate bowl, whisk the egg whites with the remaining sugar until the mixture forms soft peaks. Carefully fold the sweetened whites into the yoghurt batter. Finally, incorporate two-thirds (about 70g/2½oz) of the broken cobnuts. Spoon the mixture into the prepared tin and bake in the oven for 45–50 minutes, until a skewer inserted into the centre comes out clean. Remove the cake from the oven and allow to cool. Bash the honeycomb into small crumbs and shards and sprinkle over the cake along with the remaining cobnuts, then serve.

Blackberry & apple meringue with walnuts & elder

Sometimes it's hard to let go of the summer: warm mornings, holidays, swimming in the sea, Pimms, long lunches – and Pavlova. This Pavlova, though, is inspired by the autumn hedgerow, bursting with ripe elderberries, tart blackberries and sugary, fried windfall apples. Wet walnuts, found in markets and farm shops during the autumn period, are fresh, sweet and milky.

SERVES 8–12

a dash of sunflower or walnut oil

2 small–medium dessert apples, quartered, cored, then each quarter cut into 2 or 3 wedges

1–2 teaspoons golden caster sugar (optional)

300ml (10½fl oz) double cream

½ vanilla pod, seeds scraped

2 handfuls of blackberries

1 or 2 sprays ripe elderberries, berries picked

35g (1¼oz) shelled wet walnuts, or walnuts, or hazelnuts, roughly broken

FOR THE MERINGUE

4 egg whites

200g (7oz) golden caster sugar

Heat the oven to 120°C/235°F/gas mark 1. First, make the meringue. Place the egg whites in a large, clean bowl. Whisk with a hand-held electric whisk until they form and hold soft peaks. (You can do this in a food mixer with a whisk attachment, if you prefer.) Keeping the whisk running, add 1 large spoonful of sugar at a time, until all the sugar is incorporated. Continue to whisk for a further 6–8 minutes, until the meringue is thick, pale, smooth and glossy.

Lightly grease a sheet of baking parchment and lay it on a large (at least 30 x 30cm/12 x 12in) flat baking tray. Spoon the meringue onto the parchment, trying to make a large round with slightly peaked edges – it doesn't have to be perfect. Bake the meringue in the oven for 25–30 minutes, then turn down the heat to 90°C/185°F/gas mark ½ and bake for a further 2 hours, until the meringue has formed a crisp shell. Remove from the oven and allow to cool. (If you're not using the meringue straight away, store it in an airtight container.)

Heat the oil in a non-stick pan over a medium heat, then add the apple. If the apples are a little tart, add the caster sugar and stir. Cook the apples for 4–5 minutes, turning them over occasionally, until they have taken on a little colour and are beginning to soften. Remove the pan from the heat and allow to cool.

In a clean bowl, whisk the double cream with the vanilla seeds until thick and pillowy. Spoon the cream over the meringue base spreading it roughly out towards the edges. Arrange the cooked apple pieces over the cream. Scatter the blackberries over the top. Finally, sprinkle over the broken-up wet walnuts (or walnuts or hazelnuts) and the elderberries, and serve.

Blackberry, saffron & honey drop scones

I didn't have my first drop scone until I was in my early twenties. I was having tea with some friends who own an organic dairy farm in Dorset. The biscuit tin was empty, but within minutes a generous plateful of freshly cooked drop scones landed on the table. Made with milk from my friends' own herd of cows and with fresh eggs from the hens outside, they were cooked straight on the hot plate of the Aga and were amazing. I've made a million drop scones since then, in every which way you would care to think, but this recipe – with saffron and honey – is one I really love whenever I have a handful of blackberries to use up.

MAKES 8–10

175g (6oz) plain flour

2 teaspoons baking powder

40g (1½oz) golden caster sugar

pinch of fine sea salt

1 egg

1 small pinch of saffron strands

about 100ml (3½fl oz) milk

a few drops of vanilla extract

1 tablespoon runny honey, plus extra for serving

1 or 2 handfuls of ripe blackberries

1 large knob of butter, plus extra for serving

To make the pancake batter, place the flour into a large mixing bowl with the baking powder, sugar and salt. Crack in the egg, then add the saffron, milk, vanilla and honey. Use a whisk to combine fully. Lightly crush the blackberries and add them to the bowl, then stir through.

Melt the butter in a large non-stick frying pan over medium–high heat. Pour most of the bubbling butter into the pancake batter and stir it through to combine thoroughly. Then, one by one, add 4 generous tablespoons of batter to the pan, to make four individual pools of batter. Cook them for 1–2 minutes, until the undersides are golden, then use a small spatula to flip each drop scone over and cook the other side for 1–2 minutes until that side is golden, too. Remove the cooked drop scones to a plate or board while you repeat with the remaining batter, until it is completely used up. Serve the scones warm spread with butter and plenty more honey.

Roast parsnips with blackberries, honey chicory & rye flakes

The last of autumn's blackberries are ripe, salacious and full of flavour. Once all the berries are picked, the bramble retires back into the hedgerow, unnoticed and still for winter. It's easy to forget then how productive this thorny weed really is. In this gorgeous, colourful salad, I tumble the berries through a tray of roasted early winter parsnips, where they burst in the hot honey and olive oil, and are cut through by the bitterness of red chicory. A scattering of rye flakes adds a nutty crunch, which I really love. This is a real River Cottage favourite.

SERVES 4

4 parsnips, quartered lengthways and cored

3 tablespoons extra-virgin olive oil

2 heaped tablespoons rye flakes

2 teaspoons Dijon mustard

1 tablespoon runny honey

1 tablespoon cider vinegar

2 or 3 thyme sprigs

2 or 3 rosemary sprigs

about 100g (3½oz) blackberries

1 firm red chicory, leaves separated

salt and freshly ground black pepper

Heat the oven to 180°C/350°F/gas mark 4.

Place the parsnip quarters in a large roasting tray. Combine the olive oil, rye flakes, Dijon mustard, honey and cider vinegar in a bowl and season generously with salt and pepper. Mix well, then pour the mixture over the parsnips and tumble them to coat thoroughly. Tear over the thyme and rosemary, then place the roasting tray in the oven and roast the parsnips for 40–45 minutes, turning once or twice with a spatula, until they are tender in the middle and crisp and caramelized on the outside.

Remove the parsnips from the oven, then scatter the blackberries and chicory leaves over them. Set aside to cool for 5–10 minutes, then serve as a warm salad with fresh bread, or as an accompaniment to good sausages, duck, or pork chops.

Crab apples in brown sugar & butter

True crab apples are slightly different to the little wild apples, known as 'wildings', that grow in and around our hedgerows and along our roadsides. Proper crab apples are actually very small, like big cherries – big, very sour cherries. I've found an ancient tree on the grounds of an old estate not far from where I live. When its twisted, mossy limbs are laden with these miniature yellow apples, I'll casually scrump a bag or two. This sits perfectly easily with my conscience, as no one else seems to want them! The last time I gathered a haul, I was so enamoured with these cute little fruits, I was determined to eat them whole and in their entirety. I cooked them to bursting in plenty of brown sugar and butter. It wrapped around them like a long-lost lover, and I ate the fruit from the stalk until it was all gone.

SERVES 4

200g (7oz) ripe crab apples, or very small wild apples, stalks intact

1 knob of butter

60g (2¼oz) light soft brown sugar

good pinch of fine sea salt

Choose a shallow, heavy-based frying pan large enough to hold all your apples in a single layer. Melt the butter and sugar with the pinch of salt and 1 tablespoon of water in the pan over a medium heat to create a syrup. Bring the syrup to a gentle boil, then carefully add the apples to the pan. Simmer the apples gently in the bubbling syrup for 6–8 minutes, or until they are soft but still holding their shape. (If the syrup reduces or spits too much, add a splash more water.) Remove the pan from the heat.

Bring the apples to the table with a small jug of chilled double cream, or ice cream, and serve immediately.

Crab apple & blackberry jelly

This is a beautiful hedgerow jelly to serve with meat, particularly roast chicken, or with cheese. The crab apple gives a special flavour; the blackberries lend the jelly an almost ethereal tone. You can gather the ingredients to make this in one semi-urban or rural outdoor excursion.

MAKES 8–10 JAM JARS

about 2kg (4lb 8oz) crab apples, or small wild apples, stalks removed

2–3 handfuls of ripe blackberries

about 1kg (2lb 4oz) granulated sugar

First, sterilize your jam jars: wash them in hot soapy water, rinse them, then put them upside down in an oven at 100°C/200°F/ gas mark ½ until they are hot and dry. Or, put them through the dishwasher on its hottest setting.

Roughly chop the crab apples – skin, cores, pips and all; or pulse them in a food processor until they are broken up. Place in a large, heavy-based pan or preserving pan with the blackberries. Pour over enough water to just cover the fruit. Place the pan over a high heat and cook for 20–30 minutes, or until pulpy. If the pan looks dry at any point, add a splash more water to cover the fruit again.

Pour or ladle the fruit into a jelly bag set over a large, clean bowl. Or, you can use a large sieve lined with a clean muslin cloth. Allow the pulp to drain for 3–4 hours or even overnight. To get the clearest of jellies, avoid the temptation to squeeze or push the pulp too much – a light press with a spoon is all you need.

Measure the fruit liquid into a heavy-based pan. For every 500ml (17fl oz) liquid, add 375g (13oz) sugar. Place the pan over a low heat and stir the liquid until the sugar has dissolved, then bring it up to a rolling boil. Boil for 8–10 minutes, then start testing for setting point. To do this, turn off the heat, spoon a few drops of the jelly onto a chilled saucer (from the fridge) and return the saucer to the fridge for 2–3 minutes. Push the chilled drops of jelly with the tip of a spoon; if the surface wrinkles, you've reached setting point. If not, boil the mixture for another 3–4 minutes and test again. (If you're using a thermometer, boil until the mixture reaches 103°C/217°F.)

Allow the jelly to cool a little, then pour it into the sterilized jars and seal straight away. You can keep the jelly like this for up to 12 months.

Crab apple & fennel seed leather

This is preserving at its most simple. You dry the fruit purée until there is no moisture left, intensifying every single element of flavour. With the bite of spiky sweet fennel seeds, the resulting crab-apple leather is insanely good.

MAKES 2 SHEETS

1kg (2lb 4oz) crab apples, stalks removed and roughly chopped

2 tablespoons runny honey

2 teaspoons fennel seeds

Cook the crab apples with a splash of water in a large, heavy-based pan set over a gentle heat. Stirring regularly, cook for 45–60 minutes until the crab apples are very soft and broken down (if the fruit isn't really pulpy, continue to cook until it is). Add more water if at any point the pan looks dry. Remove from the heat and push the pulp through a mouli with a fine gauge into a clean bowl. (If you don't have a mouli, you can rub the mixture through a sieve.) Add the honey and then the fennel seeds and stir well to combine. Taste for sweetness, adding more honey if you need to.

Heat the oven to low – around 60°C/140°F/gas mark ¼ is good. Line two baking sheets with baking parchment. Divide the mixture equally between the two baking sheets, smoothing it out as evenly and as thinly as you can. Place the baking sheets in the oven for 12–14 hours until the thin layers of pulp are completely dry, even at the centre. Remove from the oven and allow to cool.

Lay out two clean pieces of baking parchment, each slightly longer and wider than the pieces of leather. Peel each leather off the baking sheet and lay it onto a prepared piece of clean parchment. Take one end of the first piece of clean parchment and roll it up with the leather inside. Repeat for the other piece of parchment and leather. The leather will keep in an airtight container for 4–5 months.

moor

m o o r | Together, we come together. I am the weather and you are the land, the peat, the pine and the heather. You stand there, all rock and swept-back tawny, like tanned leather. We meet along the bleak ridge at night and then again, sometime in the dell. I can change from kind to cruel, but you never do. You are true, like the rut, like the birds that call, like the course of rivers that once defined the way you look, your rise and fall. Wild, now kept, then burnt better. We both look to winter.

rabbit

partridge

trout

wild boar

venison

Rabbit with pappardelle

This is a very simple recipe for one of the most enjoyable pasta sauces I've ever eaten. Cook the rabbit slowly with smoked bacon, vegetables and herbs until it's tender enough to come away from the bone with ease. Flake the meat, then return it to the sauce. It's as rustic as you like, and perfect for a cold winter's night.

SERVES 4

2 tablespoons extra-virgin olive oil

6 thick rashers of smoked streaky bacon, cut into lardons

2 celery sticks, trimmed and very finely diced

1 onion, finely chopped

4 garlic cloves, peeled and thinly sliced

2 bay leaves

6 thyme sprigs

1 rosemary sprig

1 wild rabbit, jointed

about 500ml (17fl oz) chicken stock (see p. 58) or vegetable stock

1 quantity pappardelle pasta (see p. 167)

salt and freshly ground black pepper

Heat 1 tablespoon of the olive oil in a medium casserole over a medium heat. When it's hot, add the lardons and fry for 3–4 minutes, or until the bacon has given up a little fat. Add the celery, onion, garlic, bay leaves, and thyme and rosemary sprigs. Cook, stirring regularly, for 10 minutes, until the vegetables are soft and just beginning to colour.

Meanwhile, heat the remaining oil in a large non-stick frying pan over a medium–high heat. When hot, add the rabbit pieces and season them all over with salt and pepper. Fry the rabbit for 6–8 minutes on each side, or until lovely and golden all over.

Transfer the rabbit and any pan juices to the casserole of softening vegetables. Pour over the stock and bring up to a very gentle simmer. Place a lid on the casserole, leaving it just ajar, then cook on a low heat for 1½–2 hours, or until the meat is completely tender and comes easily away from the bone. If the pan looks a little dry during cooking, add a splash more stock or water.

When the rabbit is ready, remove the casserole from the heat and use a pair of tongs to transfer the rabbit pieces to a large plate. When the meat is cool enough to handle, pick it off the bone in shards and shreds and add it back to the pan. Stir everything well, and return the pan to the heat. Bring the sauce back up to a simmer and continue simmering until it has reached a consistency you're happy with (I usually leave it bubbling away for about 15–20 minutes). When it's ready, season to taste with salt and pepper.

Cook the pasta (see p. 167), drain, then drizzle with a little olive oil. Place equal amounts of pasta on each of four plates, then spoon over generous amounts of the rabbit sauce. Serve straight away.

Crispy rabbit with marjoram & lemon mayonnaise

Bring me someone who thinks they don't like rabbit, and I'll fry them up something that'll change their mind. If you're looking for an entry-level rabbit dish, this is definitely the one.

SERVES 2–4

1 wild rabbit, jointed

1 carrot, peeled and roughly chopped

1 celery stick, roughly chopped

1 onion, roughly chopped

2 bay leaves

2 thyme sprigs

sunflower oil, for frying

100g (3½oz) plain white flour, seasoned

1 large egg, beaten

100g (3½oz) fresh, coarse white breadcrumbs

salt and lemon wedges, to serve (optional)

FOR THE MAYONNAISE

2 large egg yolks

1 heaped teaspoon Dijon or English mustard

½ small garlic clove, peeled and grated

juice and zest of ½ lemon

pinch of sugar

200ml (7fl oz) sunflower oil

50ml (1½fl oz) extra-virgin olive oil

2 or 3 marjoram sprigs, leaves picked and chopped

salt and freshly ground black pepper

Start with the mayonnaise (it will keep in the fridge for several days). Place the egg yolks in a food processor with the mustard, garlic, lemon juice, sugar and some salt and pepper. Start the machine and work the ingredients together for 30–40 seconds, until everything is thoroughly combined. Combine the oils in a jug, then, with your food processor running, gently start drizzling the oil into the eggs, a few drops at a time at first, then in a steady stream. Once all the oil is in, you should have a thick mayonnaise. If it seems too thick, stir in 1–2 tablespoons of warm water. Add the marjoram and the lemon zest, and a little more seasoning, to taste. Transfer to a suitable container, cover and refrigerate.

Now for the rabbit. Place the rabbit pieces into a small–medium pan so that they fit fairly snugly. Add the carrot, celery, onion, bay leaves and thyme sprigs and cover with water. Place the pan on a high heat, and bring the contents up to a simmer. Turn down the heat and cook gently, occasionally skimming off any scum that comes to the surface, for 1½–2 hours, or until the rabbit is tender and the meat is coming away from the bone. Carefully lift out the rabbit pieces from the pan, keeping them intact, and set them aside on a plate. Allow them to cool completely, then refrigerate. Strain and reserve the stock – you can use it for any dish that needs a well-flavoured meat stock.

When you're ready to fry, fill a large heavy-based pan to about 5cm (2in) deep with sunflower oil. Heat the oil to frying hot (when a thermometer reaches 170°C/325°F, or a cube of bread takes only a minute to fizz and crisp). Toss the rabbit pieces in the seasoned flour, then turn them in the egg and then coat them in the breadcrumbs. Deep-fry the breaded rabbit for 2–3 minutes or until golden, crisp, and hot through. Serve with a sprinkling of sea salt and the mayonnaise, and a lemon wedge, if you wish.

WORKS WELL MADE WITH | chicken, pheasant

Rabbit with mustard, leeks, rosemary & cream

I once worked in a pub called The Fox. It was the most quintessential of village pubs, with worn flagstone floors, big log fires, low ceilings and good beer. Even the local mounted hunt would gallop by, almost on cue, as people arrived for lunch. My friend George was the head chef there, and after Sunday's service had come to a close, we would sit in the bar and get drunk and talk for hours about food and cooking. He showed me a very simple rabbit dish, which I've always loved. He cooked it in local cider and double cream; it was wonderfully rich. This is my version.

SERVES 2

1 tablespoon extra-virgin olive oil

1 wild rabbit, jointed

100g (3½oz) plain flour, seasoned with salt and pepper

6 rosemary sprigs

3 thyme sprigs

2 bay leaves

2 knobs of butter

2 large leeks, trimmed halved and sliced thinly

300ml (10½fl oz) cider

300ml (10½fl oz) double cream

2–3 teaspoons Dijon mustard

1 tablespoon chopped flat-leaf parsley

salt and freshly ground black pepper

Heat the oil in a large frying pan over medium−high heat. Toss the rabbit lightly in the seasoned flour, then add it to the pan, with the sprigs of rosemary and thyme and the bay. Fry for 8−10 minutes, or until the meat is golden brown on all sides and smelling delicious. Remove from the heat and set aside.

Melt the butter in a separate large, heavy-based pan over a medium heat. When it's bubbling add the leeks. Sweat them gently for 10−12 minutes, until they are soft and silky. Add the rabbit and all its pan juices and herbs, then add the cider and cream. Bring everything up to a simmer and cook, uncovered, for 1½−2 hours, or until the meat is very tender. Season with salt and pepper, then stir in the mustard. Finish with a generous sprinkling of parsley and take to the table straight away. Serve with mashed or sautéed potatoes.

Roast partridge with sage, thyme & cider

For me, partridge is every bit as good as pheasant. I always enjoy cooking it, and it seems to punch above its weight when it comes to flavour and texture. A brace carefully roasted will make a fine supper for two.

SERVES 2

2 oven-ready partridges

1 bunch of sage

1 bunch of thyme sprigs

1 garlic bulb, halved around its circumference

1 tablespoon extra-virgin olive oil

2 large knobs of butter

100ml (3½fl oz) cider

150ml (5fl oz) double cream

1 teaspoon Dijon mustard

salt and freshly ground black pepper

Heat the oven to 200°C/400°F/gas mark 6. Place the partridges in a small roasting tray, then tuck the herbs in and around the birds. Add the two halves of the garlic bulb and season well with salt and pepper. Drizzle the olive oil over the birds, place a knob of butter on top of each, then put the roasting tray in the oven. Roast the partridges for 20−25 minutes, until the skin is golden brown.

Remove the roasting tray from the oven and remove the birds to a clean plate, positioning them upside down and leaving them to rest somewhere warm. Meanwhile, place the roasting tray directly over a medium heat. To make the sauce, add the cider and bring the contents of the tray to the boil. Add the cream and stir in the mustard. Bring the sauce back to the boil, then lower the heat and simmer gently for about 5 minutes, until nicely reduced and beginning to thicken. Season the sauce with salt and pepper. Return the birds to the roasting tray along with any juices left on the plate.

Bring to the table in the tray, then place one bird on each plate and spoon over plenty of sagey, cidery sauce. Serve with buttery mash.

Barbecued partridge in yoghurt, fenugreek & black pepper

Unless we're lucky and have a dry, sunny winter, the barbecue and the game seasons seem to miss each other, which means that it doesn't seem obvious to cook game on a barbecue. It's a shame, because I think it's an approach well worth exploring — and who's to say we can't cook outside over hot coals in the winter sunshine? This recipe is a hopeful ode to a fine late-autumn and winter — or at the very least, a dryish one. The birds are spatchcocked, then spiced, then cooked cut-side down, which helps to keep the breast lovely and moist.

SERVES 2

¼ piece of 1 cinnamon stick

2 teaspoons fenugreek seeds

2 or 3 cardamom pods, seeds removed

1 teaspoon dried chilli flakes

2 teaspoons black peppercorns

2 tablespoons plain natural yoghurt, plus extra to serve (optional)

1 teaspoon fine sea salt

1 teaspoon turmeric

2 garlic cloves, peeled and grated

2 oven-ready partridges

Dry fry the cinnamon piece, fenugreek and cardamom seeds, chilli flakes and peppercorns in a small frying pan over a low heat for 3–4 minutes, until they are warm and aromatic. Tip the spices into a mill or a pestle and mortar and grind to a fairly fine texture. Place the spice mix in a small bowl and add the yoghurt, salt, turmeric and grated garlic. Mix well to combine and set aside.

Position one partridge breast-side down on a board. Using a pair of kitchen scissors, cut down each side of the backbone and remove the bone. Discard, or freeze it for your next stock. Repeat for the other bird. Using the flat of your hand, press down hard on the birds to open them out. Don't worry if you get tearing around the leg. Rub the birds all over with the spiced yoghurt, cover, and leave to marinate in the fridge for 6–8 hours or overnight.

Light the barbecue and allow the charcoal to burn down to a nice even, high heat (it's ready when you can hover your hand over the grill for only 1–2 seconds). Pass a couple of wooden kebab sticks through each bird, then place them, cut-side down on the warmed grill, and cook for 15–20 minutes, until the underside is looking coloured and crispy in places. Using the kebab sticks, flip the birds over to cook for a further 8–10 minutes, until the breast side is also golden. (You can cook them using the same technique on a medium-hot chargrilling pan, if you prefer.) Remove the birds from the direct heat, resting them at the edge of the grill for 5–10 minutes. Serve the birds whole with a tomato, onion and coriander salad. More yoghurt and some flat breads wouldn't hurt either.

Roast partridge with red cabbage, celeriac & raisins

This is roast partridge, but instead of serving it with the typical roast trimmings – like crispy roast potatoes, bread sauce and parsnip crisps – I'm serving it with a very fresh winter salad of carefully prepared and dressed raw red cabbage and celeriac, with juicy raisins. It makes for a lighter, fresher, but equally delicious accompaniment.

SERVES 2

1 good handful of raisins

juice of 1 small orange

¼ small red cabbage, tough outer leaves and dense core removed

½ celeriac (about 100g/3½oz), peeled

4 or 5 thyme sprigs, leaves stripped

2 tablespoons extra-virgin olive oil

2 oven-ready partridges

2 knobs of butter, softened

salt and freshly ground black pepper

Place the raisins in a small bowl and pour over the orange juice. Leave the raisins to plump up for 30 minutes or so.

Place the cabbage on a board and, using your sharpest knife, thinly slice into long, delicate ribbons. Use a mandoline or the same sharp knife to cut the celeriac into super-thin matchsticks.

Place the raw vegetables in a large bowl with the orange-soaked raisins, the thyme leaves and the olive oil. Season with salt and pepper and use your hands to tumble everything together. Set aside while you cook the partridges.

Heat the oven to 200°C/400°F/gas mark 6. Place the partridges, breast-side up, in a small roasting tray and spread them all over with the butter, then season with salt and pepper. Place the roasting tray in the oven and cook the birds for 25–30 minutes, until the skin is golden brown. Remove from the oven and flip the birds over onto their breasts to rest for 10–15 minutes in a warm place.

Place the birds on a board. One bird at a time, use a large, heavy knife to cut the partridges in half: place the knife on one side of the breast bone and cut down all the way through to the board. Repeat on the other side of the breastbone so that you're left with a central piece of the bird, which you can discard. Repeat the process for the other partridge.

Divide the partridge halves equally between two plates next to a serving of the salad. Trickle over some of the orangey salad dressing and spoon over any partridge roasting juices. Take to the table straight away.

Poached trout

This is a classy dish. I like to serve it while it's still warm, but not hot, as part of a fine lunch spread. It's great with crusty bread and some green leaves, and a tarragon or chive mayonnaise. It's worth spending a little time preparing the ingredients for your court-bouillon. Not only will it impart a wonderful flavour to the fish as it cooks, but you'll be left with the most delicious fish stock that you can use for soups, sauces, risottos, or anything else that calls for good fish stock. Freeze it in batches and use as required.

SERVES 4–6

2 large carrots, finely sliced

2 celery sticks, finely sliced

1 large onion, finely sliced

1 leek, trimmed and thinly sliced

1 small fennel bulb, sliced

2 or 3 garlic cloves, peeled and sliced

2 glasses of white wine

3 or 4 thyme sprigs

4 bay leaves

a few parsley stalks

1 teaspoon black peppercorns

1 teaspoon fennel seeds

1 teaspoon coriander seeds

2 teaspoons fine sea salt

1 whole trout (about 1–1.5kg/2lb 4oz–3lb 5oz), gutted and cleaned

You can make the court-bouillon immediately before poaching, or a day or two in advance (keep it stored in an airtight container in the fridge). Place all the ingredients except the fish into a large pan and cover with about 2 litres (3½ pints) water. Place the pan over a high heat and bring the contents up to a gentle simmer. Cook, simmering, for 25–30 minutes. Remove the pan from the heat and allow the stock to cool with all the vegetables and herbs in it.

Strain the stock through a sieve into a fish kettle. (Retain the vegetables as a lovely soup base – pop them in a bag and freeze them until you need them.) At this point you could add a few more aromatics, such as bay, if you like, but it's optional. Place the fish kettle over a medium heat and bring it up to a simmer. Place the fish on the trivet (the kettle insert) and lower it very gently into the poaching liquid. Turn down the heat to low and cook the fish for 15–20 minutes, or until the fish is just cooked through. I sometimes test this by pulling gently at the dorsal fin. If it comes away easily, the fish is cooked.

Lift the trivet from the kettle and remove the fish to a large serving platter, then allow it to cool a little. You can bring the fish to the table whole, or you can cut it up and serve it in portions. Serve with buttered brown bread, good mayonnaise, and a watercress salad.

Cured trout with rhubarb & rose petals

I've always loved the combination of roses and rhubarb: I've scattered fresh rose petals over pink-topped rhubarb Pavlova, and I've cooked rhubarb over the lowest of heats with rose water and honey – both times making an exquisite combination. Here, I'm integrating this gorgeous duo into a cure for fresh trout. It's a little like making a gravadlax, except I've replaced the dill with the heady, aromatic roses and the lemon with the brash acidity of rhubarb. If you've caught the fish yourself, you'll need to have a good go at the pin-boning (I use a small pair of pin-boning tweezers) to remove as many bones as possible before you cure the fish. If you're buying filleted fish, your fishmonger will have done this for you.

SERVES 8–10

100g (3½oz) rock salt or sea salt flakes

50g (1¾oz) golden caster sugar

zest of 1 lemon

2 rhubarb stems, trimmed and thinly sliced

1 teaspoon fennel seeds, lightly bashed

2 teaspoons black peppercorns, cracked

2 tablespoons rose petals

2 large trout fillets (200–300g/7–10½oz each), pin-boned

crème fraîche mixed with a squeeze of lemon juice, to serve

To make the cure, combine all the ingredients except for the fish in a bowl. Take a medium plastic or enamel tray (one that will fit in your fridge) and scatter a quarter of the cure over the base, covering an area the size of the fish fillets. Lay the fillets skin-side down on top, then scatter over the remaining cure as evenly as you can. Place the fish in the fridge, uncovered, and leave for 20–24 hours. After this time, rinse the cure off the fish under cold running water.

Pat the fish dry with a clean cotton tea towel. Lay the fish on a clean tray and place it in the fridge, uncovered, to allow it to dry out a little. I tend to leave it for a further 24 hours, or overnight.

When you're ready to serve, use a super-sharp knife to slice the fish thinly at an angle across its width, down to the skin underneath.

Serve with buttered, toasted bread and a little lemony crème fraîche on the side.

Trout with pickled cucumber, spelt & herbs

This quick, warm salad of nutty spelt grain and clean river trout always lifts my mood, particularly on a wet, wintry day. With a light air of spring about it, it provides a welcome break from the richer dishes I often prepare over the colder months of the year. It's an excellent way to use up leftover trout, or any fish for that matter. It would work beautifully with sea bass or bream, too. Be generous with the herbs, lemon and olive oil, which elevate the salad and turn it into something quite magical.

SERVES 2

½ firm cucumber, peeled

½ small red onion, finely diced

2 tablespoons cider vinegar

2 teaspoons golden caster sugar

150g (5½oz) pearled spelt

1 small bunch of mint, leaves picked, stems reserved

2 tablespoons extra-virgin olive oil

200g (7oz) cooked trout, cooled, skin and bones removed

1 small bunch of coriander

juice of ½ lemon

salt and freshly ground black pepper

Split the half cucumber in half along its length. Scoop out the seeds with the tip of a teaspoon, then slice the cucumber into 1cm (½in) half moons and place in a bowl. Add the onion, vinegar and sugar, and plenty of salt and pepper. Use a spoon to tumble the cucumber through all these ingredients and set aside to marinate.

Place the pearled spelt in a sieve and rinse well. Transfer to a pan and cover with cold water. Place the pan over a high heat and bring the liquid up to a simmer. Add the mint stems to the spelt pan so that they flavour the grain as it cooks, and cook for 15–20 minutes, until the spelt is tender but retains some bite. Drain the spelt in a colander and allow it to stand for 10–15 minutes.

In a large bowl combine the spelt with the cucumber slices and all the vinegary, sugary cucumber dressing. Add the olive oil, season well with salt and pepper, and stir to combine.

Flake the trout into large pieces and gently turn it through the warm grains. Chop all but a few of the mint leaves, and all but a few tender sprigs of the coriander. Add the chopped herbs to the salad, then spoon the salad onto a serving platter or into a bowl and drizzle over the lemon juice. Scatter over the whole herbs, then bring to the table straight away.

Roast wild boar with molasses, white beans, brown sugar & mustard

This immensely satisfying combination of boar and beans is cooked gently for hours, until the beans are soft and the meat is fork-tender. I once cooked a version of this dish in a great cast-iron pot in the glowing embers of a fire that we regularly stoked and raked as the hours of the evening passed. It turned out beautifully and we ate it around the smoky warmth drinking golden cider, with blankets around our shoulders. This version is cooked in the oven, but the principle is the same: a gentle, unrushed heat brings the best results. Mustard and molasses give the boar a dark, sweet flavour I really like. If you can't lay your hands on boar, use pork instead. You'll get something equally delicious.

SERVES 4

25g (1oz) soft brown sugar

1 tablespoon molasses

2 teaspoons crushed coriander seeds

1 teaspoon chilli flakes

1 tablespoon English mustard

1.5kg (3lb 5oz) wild boar (or pork) belly

200g (7oz) dried cannellini beans, soaked overnight in water

6 thyme sprigs

4 rosemary sprigs

8 bay leaves

1 garlic bulb, halved around its circumference

1 litre (1¾ pints) pork stock or chicken stock (see p. 58)

salt and freshly ground pepper

There's not much of a method here, which is great. By simply combining a few things and whacking them in the oven, you'll have a feast far greater than the sum of its parts.

Heat the oven to 150°C/300°F/gas mark 2. Mix the sugar, molasses, crushed coriander seeds, chilli and mustard together into a thick paste. Rub this all over the boar and set aside.

Drain the soaked beans and place them in a large, deep roasting tray that is big enough to hold the boar, too. Add the herbs, garlic and stock and give it a shake. Nestle the boar, belly down, into the beans and cover loosely with a sheet of greaseproof paper, or foil.

Place the roasting tray in the oven and cook the boar for 2½–3 hours, or until all the stock has been taken up by the beans and the boar is lovely and tender. (You may want to give everything a stir once or twice during cooking.) Remove the tray from the oven, then scoop out the boar and set aside on a plate. Season the beans in the tray with plenty of salt and pepper, giving them a good stir as you do so. Squeeze the soft garlic from its skin and work this through the beans, too.

Serve spoonfuls of the beans alongside hunks and shards of the tender boar meat. Enjoy with good bread – and good wine.

Wild boar sausages

It's worth making your own sausages – they're always infinitely better than most of the excuses for sausages you find in supermarkets. I know it's bit of a project, but it's such fun and much simpler than you might think – once you have the kit, that is. A mincer is pretty crucial, as is a sausage filler – although both may come as a combined attachment for your kitchen mixer. Or, you can buy them independently from a variety of online specialists (try weschenfelder.co.uk). Boar makes a lovely, subtle gamey sausage, but fresh pork will make something equally good.

MAKES 2KG (4LB 8OZ)
SAUSAGES

4m (13ft) hog casings
(sausage skins)

2kg (4lb 8oz) wild boar belly,
skinned and boned

200g (7oz) breadcrumbs

20g (¾oz) fine sea salt

10g (¼oz) freshly ground
black pepper

1 teaspoon soft light brown
sugar

2 tablespoons chopped
thyme leaves

1 garlic clove, peeled and
grated

100ml (3½fl oz) iced water

Wash the salt off the hog casings and leave them to soak for several hours in a bowl of fresh water. Change the water once or twice during soaking.

Cut the boar meat into small 2–3cm (¾–1¼in) cubes. Keep an eye out for any membrane or cartilage and remove it – you don't want to put any of that in your sausages.

Coarsely mince the belly meat. Then, place it in a large mixing tray or bowl. Scatter over the breadcrumbs, salt, pepper, sugar, thyme leaves and garlic, and mix thoroughly until everything is well combined. Add the iced water, and mix again. When the mixture is even, put it back through the mincer.

Pull off a golf-ball-sized piece of the sausagemeat and squash it into a small patty. Heat a small frying pan over a medium heat and quickly fry the patty, just until it's cooked through, then taste to check and adjust the seasoning, if necessary.

Place the sausagemeat in a bowl, cover and place it in the fridge while you wash your mincer and set up your sausage-filling machine. Keeping the mixture as cold as possible means the mince will go through the filler more easily and your sausages will last longer. Pass the mince through the filler and fill and link or twist off the sausages to your preferred size. Store them, covered, in the fridge for 4–5 days. Alternatively, bag them up and freeze them.

Wild boar with swede, cabbage & caraway

Lean and full of flavour, boar fillet, like cabbage, cooks in a matter of minutes in a hot pan, which is why it makes sense to fry them both at the same time. Plus, you also get better flavours (particularly when the cabbage takes on a little charring from the pan), and it saves on the washing up. I like how frying the cabbage retains some of its bite. I finish this dish with a lovely caraway and garlic butter, which lifts both the boar and the cabbage in spectacular ways.

SERVES 2

1 small swede, peeled and cut into rough cubes

2 knobs of butter

50ml (1½fl oz) double cream

½ small Savoy cabbage

1 wild boar fillet (about 400g/14oz), trimmed

1 tablespoon extra-virgin olive oil

1 garlic clove, peeled and thinly sliced

1 teaspoon caraway seeds

salt and freshly ground black pepper

Place a medium pan of salted water on a high heat and bring to the boil. Add the swede and cook for 20–30 minutes or until it's tender. Remove the pan from the heat and use a slotted spoon to transfer the swede to a blender. Add half the butter and just enough cooking liquid to allow the swede to whiz up to a velvety purée. Spoon the mixture into a clean pan, stir in the cream and season well with salt and pepper to taste. Keep warm.

Cut two thick wedges from the cabbage, each 4–5cm (1½–2in) thick at the outside edge, leaving the stem of the cabbage in place. Season the wedges and the boar fillet all over with plenty of salt and pepper. Heat the olive oil in a large, heavy-based frying pan over a medium–high heat. When it's hot, add the cabbage wedges and the fillet and cook for 4–5 minutes, turning to cook the meat and wedges evenly on all sides, until the cabbage has taken on some colour. When the cabbage is ready, turn off the heat, leaving everything in the pan and allowing the meat to rest where it is for 4–5 minutes.

While the meat is resting, melt the remaining butter in a small pan over a medium heat. When it's bubbling add the garlic and caraway seeds and cook gently for 1–2 minutes, until the garlic is just starting to toast around its edges.

Divide the swede purée equally between two plates. Cut the boar fillet into thick slices and arrange a few slices on top of each plate of purée, finish with a wedge of fried cabbage. Spoon over the garlic and caraway butter and serve straight away.

Venison cooked over a fire

Being outside is one of the most natural and beautiful ways to cook. It's definitely good for the soul — to breathe the wood smoke, to feel the heat of the embers, to use your hands in a way you don't in the kitchen.

Of course, cooking this way is not as simple as switching on the electric hob. It takes a little more thinking through, but it's far more engaging and reactive, and you connect with the ingredients in ways that elude you when you use a fan-assisted oven. You become a manager of natural heat, gauging distance over temperature over time. You unify your senses in the most wonderful ways; step-by-step recipes are set free to become simple ideas; and wind and rain become the raw elements you balance against timber or charcoal. When I cook with fire I always learn a little bit more about myself, about the ingredients, about nature and the landscape. I don't close a door on the food I'm preparing; I bring it to life, through careful tending and movement. Most of the time I keep things really simple, as here — a little salt and pepper and some rosemary. All the flavour is in the meat and the heat and the smoke.

SERVES 15–20

1 whole roe deer or small fallow deer, skinned and ready to cook (about 18–25kg/40–55lb)

1 bunch of rosemary sprigs

extra-virgin olive oil

salt and freshly ground pepper

Roe deer, somewhat smaller than fallow, sika or red deer, makes for a manageable carcass to cook over an open fire. You can usually order a carcass from your butcher or a local game dealer. If you don't have a butcher's saw, ask your butcher to spatchcock the carcass for you. If you're doing this yourself, however, cut through the middle of the spine, on the inside, mainly through the shoulders and neck, then make a cut between the haunches. You can then splay out the carcass to wire it to a brace.

I like to make my own brace on the morning of the cook. I use four lengths of sturdy, straight hazel or young coppiced ash — one (the 'upright') of around 2m (6ft) long and 8–10cm (3¼–4in) in diameter to support the carcass; the other three forming cross-bars of 1–1.5m (3–5ft) long. Cut a notch in the centre of each of the shorter lengths to help 'lock' them where they'll cross the upright. Lie the upright alongside the carcass and mark where each cross-bar will need to attach. The top cross-bar should align with the tips of the front legs, the middle with the widest part of the breast, and the lowest with the lower part of the haunches. Fix the cross-bars to the upright with heavy-duty wire, or with bolts or screws (which

I prefer, as it's a simple way to make sure they don't wobble about too much). Use wire to fix the carcass to the brace, securing the four leg shanks, fixing the spine firmly with several loops of wire around the wood of the upright. Pliers are useful to twist the wire tightly and cut away the overhang. Rub the olive oil all over the meat, and season generously all over with salt and pepper. Stick the rosemary sprigs in and around the carcass.

Make sure the fire is nice and hot before you start cooking, take a note of the wind direction and gather a decent supply of good, dry wood to burn. Stick the main pole 30cm (1ft) or so into the ground, at an angle, downwind of the fire and directly over the heat. Wedge a log under the tilt of the pole, where the upright goes into the ground, to counter the weight and support the load. Move the log forwards or backwards to adjust the cooking height of the carcass.

Cook the carcass over a high heat, feeding the fire regularly, and intermittently turning the brace through 180°. Keep your eye on the meat: make sure it's close enough to the heat to cook effectively, but not so close as to burn. Accurate cooking will involve a combination of feeding the fire and adjusting the height of the brace accordingly. Pay particular attention to the shoulders and legs, areas where the heat will take longer to penetrate.

The way you manage the fire is key. However, remember that with this type of cooking you'll always find areas of the carcass that are cooked to a greater degree than others. This is part and parcel of the technique, and something I never find a problem.

It's easy to judge when the meat is cooked to your liking. Pierce the thickest part of the carcass with a thin knife to check its internal temperature. Leave the knife in situ for a few moments, then remove it and touch it to your lip. If it burns, the meat is certainly cooked. Or, you can cut into the meat to check how it looks.

It can pay to foil-wrap some jacket potatoes and cook them in the embers of the fire to accompany the venison. Breads, salads and chutneys will all make welcome additions to the feasting table, too.

Venison stew with nettle dumplings

Venison makes a really good stew. I use the meat from the shoulder – rich, dark and deep in flavour, it responds well to slow-cooking. However, it can be lean, so here I've paired it up with some sweet-cured pancetta or bacon to add fat, and give the dish the right balance. The nettle dumplings are a cinch to make and bring an extra wild element to this already rather wild stew.

SERVES 6–8

2 tablespoons extra-virgin olive oil

2 onions, thinly sliced

2 celery sticks, washed, trimmed and thinly sliced

2 garlic cloves, peeled and thinly sliced

2 bay leaves

4 thyme sprigs

300g (10½oz) piece of pancetta or bacon, cut into 3–4cm (1¼–1½in) cubes

800g (1lb 12oz) venison shoulder, trimmed and cut into 4–5cm (1½–2in) cubes

100g (3½oz) plain flour, seasoned with salt and pepper

500ml (17fl oz) light ale

about 300ml (10½fl oz) beef stock or chicken stock (see p. 58), or water

freshly ground black pepper

FOR THE DUMPLINGS

100g (3½oz) nettle tops

250g (9oz) self-raising flour

125g (4½oz) suet

salt and freshly ground black pepper

Heat the oven to 160°C/315°F/gas mark 2–3. Heat half the oil in a large casserole over a medium heat, then add the onion, celery, garlic, bay leaves and thyme sprigs. Sweat the onions, stirring, for 8–10 minutes, until soft. Meanwhile, heat the remaining oil in a large heavy-based frying pan over a high heat. When it's hot, turn down the heat and gently fry the pancetta or bacon, until the fat has rendered and the meat is golden. Transfer to the casserole, leaving the frying pan on the heat. Toss the venison in the seasoned flour, then add to the frying pan, in batches, transferring each batch to the casserole as soon as it is well coloured, about 4–6 minutes. Stir the casserole contents, then pour the ale over, along with enough stock or water to cover by 2–3cm (¾–1¼in). Season with pepper. Bring up to a simmer, then transfer to the oven, leaving the lid just ajar, and cook for 2½–3 hours until the meat is very tender.

Shortly before the venison is ready, make the dumplings. Bring a medium pan of water to the boil and add the fresh nettle tops. Cook for 2 minutes until wilted, then drain and allow to cool. Squeeze all the water from the cooked nettles into a bowl and retain. Chop the wilted leaves relatively finely. Mix the flour, suet and nettle together with some salt and pepper. Stir in enough cooled nettle water to form a soft dough – about 150–200ml (5–7fl oz). Using your hands, form the mixture into 10 spherical dumplings. Take the stew from the oven and remove the lid. Distribute the dumplings evenly over the surface of the stew, replace the lid fully, and return the stew to the oven. Allow to cook for a further 20 minutes, then remove the lid and cook for a further 10–15 minutes, until the top of each dumpling has taken on a little colour. Remove the stew from the oven and serve with buttered greens or a lovely mixed salad.

Seared venison with anise, rhubarb & honey

Honey and a little sugar soften – but only soften – the acidity of the rhubarb in this colourful dish. I like a slight sharpness, particularly when rhubarb pairs with venison loin, the most tender of all cuts to be found on the deer. It works in the same way a Bramley apple sauce works with pork, or the way a bittersweet plum sauce complements duck. Star anise forms a delicate bridge of spice between rhubarb and venison, as it is equally compatible with both.

SERVES 4

2–3 rhubarb stems (about 300g/10½oz altogether), trimmed and cut into 3–4cm (1¼–1½in) pieces

2 tablespoons honey

juice of ½ an orange

2 teaspoons golden caster sugar

1 star anise, roughly broken

400–500g (14oz–1lb 2oz) venison loin, trimmed and ready to cook

2 tablespoons extra-virgin olive oil

1 handful of small chard leaves or other delicate salad leaf

salt and freshly ground black pepper

Heat the oven to 120°C/235°F/gas mark 1. Place the rhubarb pieces in a medium, shallow baking dish and drizzle over the honey, add the orange juice, and scatter over the sugar and star anise.

Cover the dish loosely with a piece of greaseproof paper and place the rhubarb in the oven for 20–25 minutes, or until the rhubarb is soft but not broken down. Remove from the oven and set aside.

Meanwhile, season the venison all over with salt and pepper. Heat 1 tablespoon of the olive oil in a medium pan over a high heat. When it's really hot, add the venison loin. Cook, turning regularly, for 4–5 minutes for medium–rare. Remove the meat from the pan and allow it to rest somewhere warm for 3–4 minutes.

Divide the rhubarb equally between four large plates, reserving the syrup in the bottom of the dish. Cut the loin into thick slices and lay it on and around the rhubarb. Scatter over the chard or other salad leaves, and drizzle over the reserved honey-and-anise syrup. Finish with a drizzle of the remaining olive oil and serve straight away.

harbour

harbour

Protected boats behind steel, massive stone and brined oak, hard weathered-down grains. Cold salt, the launch, the open deck, the hulk laid up. Beautiful diesel and the whip of the rig, smoke and nets. Buoys, banks, the leading flash of greens and reds. Bells in the dark, marks, hauling nets, cigarettes and dawn mackerel trips. Great bounties and empty holds. Hard hands and the fisherman, the Beaufort, tall tales, bass scales, conger heads below the ebb, the peace of high water.

cod

pollack

brill

squid

scallops

Cod with salsify, thyme & butter

Salsify makes the perfect accompaniment to fresh cod and couldn't be easier to prepare: I like to serve a salad of bitter leaves dressed with a squeeze of lemon – it cuts through the richness of the fish perfectly. Here, though, this unusual winter vegetable has decadence... buttery decadence. The low, slow cooking renders it unctuous and giving; while the garlic and thyme help to make it unbelievably tasty.

SERVES 4

800g (1lb 12oz) salsify, peeled

150g (5½oz) butter, cut into 1cm (½in) cubes

4 garlic cloves, peeled and thinly sliced

zest of ½ lemon

1 small bunch of thyme sprigs

200ml (7fl oz) chicken (see p. 58) or vegetable stock, or water

4 cod fillets (about 150g/5½oz each), skin on

salt and freshly ground black pepper

Heat the oven to 150°C/300°F/gas mark 2. Place the salsify in a medium roasting tray, dot the butter all over the salsify, along with the sliced garlic, lemon zest and the thyme sprigs. Pour in the stock or water and season well with salt and pepper. Cover the tray tightly with foil, crimping the edges, to keep in the steam as the salsify cooks. Place the salsify in the oven for about 2 hours, shaking the tray once or twice during this time, until it is lovely and tender. Remove the tray from the oven and remove the foil.

Turn up the oven to 200°C/400°F/gas mark 6. Season the cod all over with salt and pepper and set it in and among the salsify, turning it through the melted butter in the tray as you do so. Return the tray to the oven and cook the fish and the salsify for 15 minutes, or until the cod is just cooked through.

Place some salsify and a piece of cod on each plate, then spoon over the hot, well-flavoured butter and serve straight away.

Slashed and roast cod with chorizo, rosemary & purple-sprouting broccoli

Roasting a whole fish is so easy – it's the sort of thing I do when I'm pushed for time. A fish big enough for four or six people won't take much longer than 30 minutes to prepare and cook, making it an incredibly practical and stress-free way to feed a crowd. I always like to bring the whole fish to the table and let people help themselves, each lifting their favourite bits of flesh from the bone. You can keep roasted fish as simple as you like, but here I'm getting in a handful of cod's great friends: hot paprika-spiked chorizo, sliced garlic, and rosemary. As the fish comes out of the oven, I tumble some purple-sprouting broccoli through all that goodness in the tray.

SERVES 4–6

1 whole cod (about 1.5–2kg/3lb 5oz–4lb 8oz), scaled, gutted and cleaned

4 tablespoons extra-virgin olive oil, plus extra for oiling

250g (9oz) good-quality air-dried chorizo sausage

juice and zest of 1 lemon

2 garlic cloves, peeled and thinly sliced

2 or 3 rosemary sprigs

400–500g (14oz–1lb 2oz) purple-sprouting broccoli

1 knob of butter

salt and freshly ground black pepper

Heat the oven to 200°C/400°F/gas mark 6. Dry the fish well inside and out. Use a sharp knife to slash each side of the fish 3 or 4 times, on each side, cutting all the way down to the bone, this will help the heat work into the fish and speed up the cooking time a little.

Oil a shallow roasting tray big enough to accommodate your fish. Place the cod on the tray then season it all over with salt and pepper and rub in the olive oil. Place the tray in the oven and cook the fish for an initial 10 minutes.

In the meantime, bring a pan of salted water to the boil for the broccoli, but don't put it in just yet. Peel the papery skin from the chorizo and cut it into 1–2cm (½–¾in) rounds.

Remove the roasting tray from the oven and scatter over the chorizo, lemon zest and garlic slices, and the rosemary sprigs. Try to wedge a little bit of everything into the slashes in the cod and to tuck a little bit under the fish, too. Return the roasting tray to the oven for a further 10 minutes, or until the fish is just cooked through. (If the white meat lifts away from the bone, it's cooked.)

While the fish is cooking, boil the purple-sprouting broccoli for 2–4 minutes, until the stalks are just tender. Drain well, then when the fish is ready, add it to the tray, along with the butter and lemon juice. Turn the broccoli through the oily chorizo and garlic, taking care not to break it up. Bring the tray to the table with a stack of warm plates, some roast or sauté potatoes and a good salad.

Fried cod with ginger, beetroot, orange & sesame

Cod is an extremely versatile, naturally flavoursome, firm-fleshed white fish, which you can cook in all sorts of exciting ways and with all manner of different ingredients. It can hold its own against some pretty big flavours. I like what the beetroot and orange get up to here – they work so well together, but they also have the means to take all the other ingredients along with them.

SERVES 2

2 teaspoons sesame oil

2 cod fillets (about 150g/5½oz each), skin on

1 small beetroot, cut into thin matchsticks

2 garlic cloves, peeled and thinly sliced

2.5cm (1in) piece of root ginger, peeled and very thinly sliced

½–1 red chilli, deseeded and thinly sliced

2 tablespoons tamari or soy sauce

juice of 1 orange

2 teaspoons runny honey

1 tablespoon sesame seeds, plus extra for scattering (optional)

2 teaspoons cider vinegar

Heat the sesame oil in a medium, non-stick pan over a medium–high heat. Lightly season the cod with salt and add this skin-side down to the pan. Cook the fish for 3–4 minutes, then scatter the beetroot matchsticks, and sliced garlic, ginger and chilli into the pan, so they start to cook nice and quickly. Give them 1–2 minutes to sizzle, before you flip the fish fillets over. Add the tamari, orange juice, honey, sesame seeds and cider vinegar. At this point the cod should be cooked through, but if it's not quite there give it a little longer, adding a dash of water to the pan if it looks like the liquid is reducing too far.

When the fish is cooked through (when the translucent flesh becomes fully opaque), carefully remove the fish to warmed plates. Continue to simmer the sauce for a further 30–40 seconds to thicken slightly. Spoon the contents of the pan over each serving of fish and serve immediately with an extra scattering of sesame seeds, if you like.

You can serve the cod with rice or, as I sometimes do, some sprouted lentils.

Pollack & oxtail

We are so very different you and I. You are dark, broken down and deep;
tender beyond words. I am pale and as fresh as cold water. I am fragile and
need you to hold me up and carry me.

I've always loved this simple coupling of ingredients. They are so very different and it
charms me to think how they work so harmoniously together.

SERVES 4–6

1kg (2lb 4oz) oxtail, cut into
pieces (ask your butcher to
do this)

1 tablespoon extra-virgin
olive oil or beef dripping

2 onions, halved and finely
sliced

2 small celery sticks,
trimmed and thinly sliced

2 garlic cloves, peeled and
thinly sliced

pared zest of ½ small
orange

3 bay leaves

4 juniper berries, lightly
bashed

2 thyme sprigs

150ml (5fl oz) red wine

500ml (17fl oz) good-quality
beef stock

4–6 pollack fillets (about
120–150g/4¼–5½oz each)

salt and freshly ground
black pepper

Season the oxtail all over with salt and pepper. Heat the oil or
dripping in a large heavy-based casserole over a medium heat.
Add the oxtail pieces and cook, turning regularly, for about
8–10 minutes, until they have a deep colour and are starting
to crisp. Remove the oxtail from the pan and set aside. Add the
onions, celery, garlic, orange zest, bay leaves, juniper, and thyme
sprigs to the pan and cook, stirring, for 10 minutes, until the
onions are soft.

Return the oxtail pieces to the pan, arranging them in a tight,
single layer. Pour over the wine and the stock so that the liquid
covers the oxtail by 1–2cm (½–¾in), and bring it up to a simmer.
Place a lid on the pan and cook over a very low heat for 3–4 hours,
or until the oxtail meat falls off the bone. If at any point the pan
looks a bit dry, add a dash of water or more stock to cover the meat.

Remove the oxtail pieces from the pan and allow them to cool a
little. Use a large spoon to skim off the excess fat from the surface
of the sauce, reserving a few spoonfuls of the fat for frying the fish.
Turn up the heat, then reduce the sauce by half – it should thicken
and become full of flavour. Adjust the seasoning. Return the oxtail
to the sauce, either in whole pieces or flaked off the bone.

Set a large non-stick pan over a medium–high heat. Season the
fish all over with salt and pepper. Heat the reserved fat in the pan
and when hot add the fish, skin-side down. Cook for 3–5 minutes,
depending on its thickness, then turn the fillets over and fry for
1–2 minutes, until the flakes separate when pressed lightly with a
fork, which indicates the fish is cooked. Spoon the warm oxtail and
plenty of sauce onto the plates. Lift the fish from the pan and place
alongside. Serve straight away.

Salted pollack with potatoes, cream & marjoram

This makes such a good supper – it is so much more than fish and potatoes. You can take out the dried salted fish and on the surface it would look much the same – but underneath the crisp and caramelized potato topping it wouldn't have the extraordinary intensity that the salted pollack brings. To make your own salted fish, cover a large fillet of very fresh pollack, cod or other white fish in fine salt and leave it the fridge for 48 hours. Wash the salt off the fish and hang it to dry somewhere cool and airy (a porch, lean-to or shed is perfect). It will hang for many weeks, even months. I tend to do this in the autumn or winter when there are fewer flies. When you're ready to use it, soak it for 12 to 18 hours in several changes of fresh cold water.

SERVES 6–8

1kg (2lb 4oz) white floury potatoes, such as Desirée or Maris Piper

1 large onion, thinly sliced

4–6 garlic cloves, peeled and thinly sliced

2 tablespoons chopped marjoram, plus a couple of marjoram flower stems for topping (optional)

500ml (17fl oz) double cream

300–400g (10½–14oz) thoroughly soaked salted pollack or cod fillets, skinned and sliced into small pieces

salt and freshly ground black pepper

Heat the oven to 160°C/315°F/gas mark 2–3. Peel and slice the potatoes thinly into 2–3cm (¾–1¼in) rounds. Place the slices in a large bowl with the onions, garlic and marjoram, and plenty of black pepper (it may not need salt as the fish will bring this to the mix). Place the cream into a small pan over a medium heat and bring it up to a simmer. Pour the hot cream over the potatoes and turn well to combine.

Place a relatively neat layer of overlapping potatoes in the bottom of a large round dish about 20–25cm (8–10in) in diameter and 5cm (2in) deep. Scatter over some of the sliced fish, then make a second layer of overlapping potatoes. Continue until you have used up the fish, finishing with a layer of potato on top. Pour over all the remaining cream from the bowl. Top with a couple of marjoram flower stems, which I think look lovely and dry brittle as glass in the oven – but of course they're not essential.

Place the dish in the oven and bake the layered potato-and-fish pie for 1 hour, pressing the potatoes down firmly once or twice during cooking using a spatula, until the potatoes are tender, the top layer is golden and the sauce is bubbling. Remove the dish from the oven and allow it time to settle. It will be much better, and still nice and hot, after 30 minutes of sitting. Serve with a green salad or steamed, lemony purple-sprouting broccoli.

Whole roast pollack with garden herbs & pancetta

This is another beautifully simple one-tray supper that is as big on flavour as it is quick to prepare. You can buy really good-quality pancetta made from free-range pork in independent delis and at deli counters in supermarkets. Look out for the stuff with a generous marbling of fat, which brings so much flavour and sweetness to the fish. And use plenty of herbs – they are so fantastic with fish, the more the merrier. Don't chop them, just throw them all in. They become crunchy and delicate and add extra dimension to this rustic roast.

SERVES 2

1 whole pollack (1–1.5kg/2lb 4oz–3lb 5oz), scaled, gutted and cleaned

100g (3½oz) fatty pancetta, cut into chunky lardons

1 small bunch of mixed herbs, such as bay leaves, rosemary, sage, thyme, parsley leaves, fennel tops, chives

1 tablespoon extra-virgin olive oil

salt and freshly ground black pepper

Heat the oven to 200°C/400°F/gas mark 6. Select a roasting tray that provides a snug fit for your fish. Scatter over the pancetta pieces and the hard perennial herbs (the bay leaves, rosemary, sage and thyme). Drizzle over the olive oil, then season well with salt and pepper. Place the fish in the oven and cook for 25 minutes, until the fish is cooked through (you can test this by inserting the tip of a small paring knife into the thickest part of the fish and seeing if the flesh comes away from the bone).

While the fish is roasting, prepare the tender herbs (the parsley, fennel tops, and chives) ready to scatter over the fish when it comes out of the oven: slice the chives thinly, and chop the parsley leaves and fennel tops, then put them in a bowl and combine thoroughly.

As soon as the fish is cooked remove it from the oven and scatter over these herbs while it's still in the tray.

Bring the whole roasting tray to the table. Use a knife and small spatula to lift generous portions of fish from the bone and place it onto the individual plates. Spoon over any loose herbs that remain in the tray, as well as the crisped pancetta and any well-flavoured, rich, herby roasting juices. Serve straight away with hunks of good-quality bread, new potatoes and a nice green salad.

Whole roast brill with celeriac & hedgehog mushrooms

This is the kind of bold, early winter supper dish that makes me really happy. It's unfussy cooking at its very best, with all the ingredients cooked together in the biggest roasting tray you can muster. If you can't find hedgehog mushrooms use chestnut or portobello mushrooms instead.

SERVES 4

2 knobs of butter

1 whole brill (about 1.5–2kg/3lb 5oz–4lb 8oz), gutted and cleaned

2 or 3 garlic cloves, peeled and sliced

2 tablespoons extra-virgin olive oil, plus extra for oiling

400–500g (14oz–1lb 2oz) celeriac, peeled and cut into 3–4cm (1¼–1½in) cubes

about 250–300g (9–10½oz) hedgehog mushrooms (enough to fill a small basket), cleaned

1 small bunch of parsley, leaves picked and chopped

salt and freshly ground black pepper

Heat the oven to 220°C/425°F/gas mark 7. Oil a large, flat roasting tray big enough to accommodate your fish, mushrooms and celeriac. Rub the base of the tray with half the butter, then season with some salt and pepper. Place the fish in the tray, scatter over the garlic slices, drizzle the fish with the olive oil, then give it a massage and season all over with salt and pepper. Scatter the celeriac cubes around the fish and add the mushrooms to the tray. I tend to leave them more or less whole, unless they're really big, as they get cooked for the same amount of time as the fish and celeriac.

Dot the celeriac, mushrooms and fish with the remaining butter and season with a little more salt and pepper. Place the tray in the oven, and cook for 25 minutes, until the fish is cooked through (you can test this by inserting the tip of a small paring knife into the thickest part of the fish and seeing if the flesh comes away from the bone). Turn the mushrooms and celeriac once halfway through cooking.

Remove the tray from the oven and allow the fish to rest for 4–5 minutes before scattering with the chopped parsley and taking to the table straight away. Allow everyone to help themselves to a serving of fish and a scoop of the vegetables, straight from the tray.

Brill with sorrel sauce

I really like the flavour of sorrel: it's sharp and green and appley-sour. Common sorrel is easy to grow at home, but you'll also find it growing wild, small and spear-shaped, in grassy fields and grazing land. The zesty acidity of wild sorrel works beautifully in salads and it makes a sauce that works wonderfully with fish, particularly brill. A version of this recipe has been on the menu at a fish restaurant in Dorset that I've been going to since I was a child. My mum still orders it every time she goes to eat there.

SERVES 4

4 brill fillets (120–150g/
4¼–5½oz each), skin on

1 tablespoon extra-virgin
olive oil

4 bay leaves

2–4 thyme sprigs

2 garlic cloves, skin on and
bashed

1 small knob of butter

FOR THE SAUCE

1 large knob of butter

1 shallot, halved and very
finely diced

100ml (3½fl oz) fish stock
or water

1 large bunch of sorrel
(about 150g/5½oz), stalks
removed (I use cultivated
sorrel)

150ml (5fl oz) double cream

salt and freshly ground
black pepper

First, make the sorrel sauce. Melt the butter in a small pan over a medium heat. When it is bubbling, add the shallot and cook, stirring regularly, until it is soft and sweet. Pour over the stock, bring up to a simmer and watch it bubble away gently until the liquid has almost disappeared (about 2 minutes). Cut the sorrel leaves into rough ribbons and throw them into the pan. Give the sorrel a stir with a wooden spoon once or twice in the pan to ensure the leaves are nicely wilted. Add the cream, stir, and bring the sauce up to a simmer. Cook for 1–2 minutes, until the sauce has thickened slightly. Season with salt and pepper, then remove from the heat, cover and set aside.

Season the fish all over. Heat the olive oil, along with the bay, thyme and garlic, in a large non-stick frying pan over a medium–high heat. Place the pieces of seasoned brill skin-side down into the pan. Cook for 5–6 minutes, until the fish has cooked at least three-quarters of the way up its edge. Use a spatula to turn over the fish, cook for 1 minute more, then add the butter and remove the pan from the heat. Rest the fish in the pan for 1 minute while the butter melts.

Place one brill fillet onto each plate with the sauce alongside. It's lovely served with a bowl of crisp sauté potatoes.

Brill with anchovies, cream & rosemary

It's difficult to explain just how brilliant the combination in this sauce is: big and totally rounded. When you eat it, it's like the ingredients were invented only for this dish. It almost makes you sad because it's so good! I love it with brill, but in truth it's delicious with just about anything.

SERVES 5

5 brill fillets (120–150g/
4¼–5½oz each), skin on

1 tablespoon extra-virgin
olive oil

8–12 anchovies in oil

1–2 medium–hot dried
chillies, deseeded and sliced

8 garlic cloves, peeled and
thinly sliced

4–6 rosemary sprigs, leaves
roughly torn from the stem

2 thyme sprigs (optional)

75ml (2¼fl oz) double cream

salt and freshly ground
black pepper

Season the brill fillets well with salt and pepper. Heat the oil in a large non-stick frying pan over a medium–high heat. When it's hot, add the brill skin-side down. Fry for 4–5 minutes, or until the fish has cooked at least three-quarters of the way up its edge. Remove the pan from the heat and use a spatula to remove the fish to a plate. Return the pan to the heat and add the anchovies, chilli, garlic and rosemary, and the thyme, if using.

Use a spatula to move the ingredients around the pan for 2–3 minutes, until the anchovies start to break down and the garlic and rosemary smell fragrant, then return the brill to the pan, this time skin-side up. Give the pan a shake, then add the cream along with 2 tablespoons of water and bring the liquid up to a simmer. Cook for 4–6 minutes, until the sauce is thick and bubbling. Give the sauce a taste and adjust the seasoning if you need to. Remove from the heat.

Place one piece of fish on each plate, spoon over some sauce and serve straight away with good-quality rustic bread and a dressed green salad, or with buttery mash and steamed purple-sprouting broccoli.

Raw squid with lemon, apple, chervil & nasturtium leaves

I first made this dish during an unusually intense, beer-fuelled late-night cook-off in a Copenhagen kitchen. It went down really well with the judges, and, I think, helped to clinch my victory. I will assume that not many people reading this recipe will have tried raw squid, but let me assure you the flavour and texture are absolutely wonderful. It has a subtle creaminess and a tenderness you don't get when you cook it. Don't be nervous of it either – it's no different to eating sashimi; just use the freshest squid you can lay your hands on and have a go. I serve it with sweet apple and peppery nasturtiums, a little lemon and my best extra-virgin olive oil. Altogether an excellent combination.

SERVES 4

2 dessert apples

1 large handful of nasturtium leaves, plus extra to serve

zest of ¼ lemon and juice of 1 whole, plus extra juice for serving

2 tablespoons extra-virgin olive oil, plus extra for serving

apple juice or water, for loosening the purée (optional)

1 very fresh squid body (150–200g/5½oz–7oz), cleaned

1 small bunch of chervil

salt and freshly ground black pepper

Peel one of the apples, then quarter and core it. Place it in a blender along with the nasturtium leaves, the lemon zest, half the lemon juice, 1 tablespoon of the olive oil, and a little salt and pepper. Blitz the ingredients until they form a smooth purée. (You can do this using a stick blender, if you prefer.) You may have to add a dash of apple juice or water to help it on its way.

Cut down one side of the squid's tubular body and open it out. Use your sharpest knife to scrape any thin membrane from the surface of the flesh. You want the squid to be beautifully smooth before you slice it. Starting at the widest end, slice long, super-thin lengths of squid from the body. They should look like short lengths of delicate, almost translucent tagliatelle pasta.

Place the squid slices in a bowl, allowing 30–40g (1–1½oz) squid per person. Drizzle over the remaining olive oil and lemon juice and season lightly with salt and pepper. Turn together well.

Using your sharpest knife again, cut very thin rounds from top to bottom of the remaining apple – you'll need a couple of slices for each person. Arrange these in the base of each bowl. Put equal amounts of squid on top, then dot over the nasturtium and apple purée, and finish with a few sprigs of chervil and a few nasturtium leaves. Finally give everything a final spritz of lemon juice, a drizzle of olive oil and a sprinkling of salt and pepper. Serve straight away.

Fried squid with garlic & parsley

This is such a classic way to prepare and cook squid. It's also, quite possibly, one of the most delicious ways to eat it — which is why I had to get it in here somehow. I find small-to-medium-sized squid work best, as really big ones can be a little tough (but, hey, it's good to know what you're eating sometimes). I worked with a chef who used to stuff the bodies of fresh squid with scrunched-up foil, then steam them until butter-tender. Once he'd chilled them, he would cut them into rings and fry them in the traditional way. His technique offered consistency for sure, but all the squid's fantastic flavourful character and textural appeal had been steamed right out of them. I prefer to keep it much more real.

SERVES 6–8 TAPAS STYLE

50g (1¾oz) cornflour

50g (1¾oz) plain flour

500g (1lb 2oz) whole squid, cleaned, body cut into 1cm (½in) rings, tentacles left whole (or halved if large)

500ml (17fl oz) sunflower oil, for deep frying

2 tablespoons extra-virgin olive oil

2 tablespoons chopped flat-leaf parsley

½ garlic clove, peeled and grated

salt and freshly ground black pepper

lemon wedges, to serve (optional)

Combine the cornflour and plain flour in a bowl and season well with salt and pepper.

Pour the oil into a wok or large saucepan so that it comes halfway up the sides of pan, then place the pan over a medium–high heat. If you're using a thermometer, heat the oil to 180°C/350°F. If not, you can check the oil is at the right temperature by dropping in a small cube of bread — after 1 minute, it should turn golden and crisp.

Take a handful of squid rings and tentacles and turn them through the flour to coat thoroughly. Then, place them in a sieve and shake off the excess flour so that it falls back into the bowl.

When all the squid pieces are coated, gently add them a handful at a time to the hot oil. Fry for 3–4 minutes, until they're golden and crisp, then lift them out with a slotted spoon onto kitchen paper. Allow the oil in the pan to heat back up again and repeat with the remaining squid, until all the rings and tentacles are cooked.

Combine the olive oil with the chopped parsley and garlic and mix well.

Heap the squid into a large bowl, or divide it between several smaller plates. Spoon over the parsley-and-garlic dressing and serve sprinkled with salt, and with some fresh lemon wedges for squeezing, if you like.

Barley paella with squid & pheasant

This charming take on classic paella uses pheasant instead of chicken and locally grown pearl barley instead of a more typical white rice. It all happens in one pan, so it's a great one to cook outside over a fire and eat with family and friends. I pack everything I need into a rucksack, including a decent stock decanted into a large plastic bottle, and head to the beach. Try to find a really good, smoky chorizo, deep red with wine and paprika — it goes so well with both the pheasant and the squid. (I've made the same dish with rabbit and that's stunning too.) You can carefully cut the meat off the bone if you like, but I like to leave the thighs and the drumsticks whole. It gives everyone something to pick up and hold in their hands.

SERVES 6

1 pheasant, jointed

100ml (3½fl oz) extra-virgin olive oil, plus extra for serving

200g (7oz) good-quality chorizo, sliced into thick rounds

1 red pepper, halved deseeded and cut into strips

2 onions, thinly sliced

4 garlic cloves, peeled and thinly sliced

400g (14oz) pearl barley

2 glasses of white wine

2 litres (3½ pints) pheasant or chicken stock (see p. 58)

2 pinches of saffron strands

500g (1lb 2oz) whole squid, cleaned, body cut into 1cm (½in) rings, tentacles cut into 2 or 3 bits

1 large bunch of flat-leaf parsley, chopped

juice of 1 lemon, plus extra wedges for serving

salt and freshly ground black pepper

First, cut the jointed pheasant breasts into 4 pieces, and separate the thighs and drumsticks. Then, place a large paella pan, or your biggest casserole over a medium heat or the embers of a glowing fire. Add half the olive oil followed by the pheasant pieces and the chorizo. Season with salt and pepper and fry for 4–5 minutes, until all the meat has taken on a little colour. Scatter in the red pepper, onion and garlic and cook for a further 5–6 minutes. Now add the pearl barley and fry for 1–2 minutes, stirring once or twice to coat the grains. Add the wine and bring the liquid up to a simmer. Add the stock and the saffron and cook, stirring regularly to prevent sticking, for 25–35 minutes, until most of the stock has been absorbed by the grain.

At this point add the well-cleaned squid and the parsley. Stir well, and cook for a further 4–5 minutes, until the pearl barley is tender but still has a little texture. If you feel it is too al dente, add a splash of water to the pan and cook for 4–5 minutes more. When you're happy, turn off the heat or remove the paella from the fire. Drizzle over the lemon juice, taste and adjust the seasoning with plenty of salt and pepper. Allow the paella to rest, covered, for 5–10 minutes.

Serve with lemon wedges, a little more olive oil, good bread and good wine.

Raw scallops with dill, red onion, lemon & olive oil

This gentle and refined scallop dish is more of a ceviche than a tartare. With a tartare, the meat or fish is completely raw, but with a ceviche it is 'cooked' – effectively – by the acidity of the citrus juice. Here, the scallop sits in the lemon juice, but only for about 10 minutes, which I think is more than enough. The recipe has a slight Scandinavian feel to it, which takes it into new territory – as far as ceviche goes anyway.

SERVES 2

2 or 3 large, very fresh scallops (about 150g/5½oz prepared weight)

juice and zest of ½ large lemon

½ very small red onion, very finely diced

3 or 4 dill sprigs, chopped, reserving a few small tips to garnish

2 tablespoons extra-virgin olive oil

salt and freshly ground black pepper

Make sure your scallops are super-fresh for this dish. I tend to buy live ones, in the shell, then cut and prepare them myself. However, your fishmonger will happily do this for you, if you prefer. To do it yourself, take a thin-bladed knife, such as a filleting knife, and hold the shell upright, with the rounded edge downward on the board and the hinge at the top. If you're right-handed, the flat side of the shell should face to your right (and to your left, if you're left handed). Find an opening as near to the top edge of the shell as possible and ease in the knife tip. Keep the knife as tight to the flat of the shell as possible and cut down through the muscle at the point it meets the shell. This will allow you to open the scallop.

Run the tip of the knife under the scallop and lift it out of the lower part of the shell onto a board. Remove the orange-coloured roe, the translucent strip of frill and the black gut sack at the back of the muscle. Peel away the very fine membrane that runs around the scallop's edge so that you're left with pure white muscle. Save the roe for frying off separately and freeze the frills for fish stock (they have a lot of flavour). Repeat for all the scallops.

Dice the scallop meat into large pea-sized pieces and combine with the lemon juice and zest, and the diced red onion, chopped dill and olive oil. Season with a little salt and pepper and turn gently together. Let the scallops sit in the lemon for 10 minutes, then serve straight away with a scattering of the reserved dill and the juices from the bowl.

Grilled scallops with green peppercorns & garlic

When I was 12 years old I got my first job in a pub. I was paid £1 an hour to wash up. I know, £1! They served really good food there, and occasionally I got to taste it. One dish that drove me completely crazy was the grilled scallops in garlic butter. The chef sent them out in the shell, straight from the ferocity of the grill to the table, still bubbling. The smell of the butter and garlic would make my little tummy turn cartwheels in hopeful anticipation. Annoyingly, I never did get to try them, but hey, at least I was getting paid. This dish, and the smell as it cooks, reminds me of those first kitchen shifts I did as a kid. This is a really simple recipe to put together. I've added a dash of cream here, and green peppercorns, which I love with seafood.

SERVES 2 AS A STARTER

6 scallops, white meat removed from the shells (see p. 278)

1 knob of butter

2 garlic cloves, peeled and thinly sliced

2 teaspoons green peppercorns

2 thyme sprigs

2–3 tablespoons double cream

salt and freshly ground black pepper

Heat the grill to its highest setting. Place the prepared scallops in a solid little tray or dish that will sit happily under the grill. Dot the butter over and around them, along with the sliced garlic, green peppercorns and thyme sprigs. Season well with salt and pepper.

Place the dish under the grill. It wants to be pretty close to the flame or element. Grill the scallops for 2–3 minutes on the first side, then flip them over, add the cream, give the dish a little shuffle to mix it all up, and return to the grill to cook for a further 2 minutes, until the scallops are cooked through and the sauce is bubbling deliciously.

Bring the scallops to the table with hunks of good bread for mopping up the sauce.

Scallops cooked in fire embers with seaweed butter

I can't think of many other ingredients that come complete with their own little frying pan that is both beautiful and conducts the heat so well. For this recipe you'll need to buy your scallops in the shell, or at least in the half shell, because they cook in the shells themselves. I do this directly in the embers of a fire – it's brilliant fun and quick, and the scallops taste so good with a hint of wood smoke and edge of burnt butter. I've given a method for making your own butter, a project I find really rewarding, but of course normal stuff will be absolutely fine. I add dried seaweed and a hint of garlic – they bring a fitting depth that complements the scallops perfectly.

SERVES 2

280ml (9½fl oz) double cream (or 100g/3½oz butter)

2 tablespoons dried seaweed flakes

1 small garlic clove, peeled and finely grated

good pinch of sea salt

6–8 large scallops in their shells

freshly ground black pepper

To make the butter, pour the cream into a bowl and whisk until it starts to thicken then split. Then, use a wooden spoon to beat the cream and drive out the buttermilk. Once the butter granules begin to bind, dip your hands in icy water, then squeeze the butter together to get out as much buttermilk as possible and form a solid mass. Save the buttermilk for soups, smoothies or bread.

In a bowl place the butter with the seaweed flakes, the grated garlic and the salt, add black pepper to season, then beat together. Place the flavoured butter on a sheet of greaseproof paper and form into a rough cylinder. Roll it up in the paper and refrigerate.

Open the scallops (see p. 278), but leave the roe attached to the muscle. Place a scallop in each half shell, remove the butter from the fridge and break a generous disc over the scallop.

Level out the hot embers of the fire with a stick or poker, then place the scallop shells onto them. The scallops will heat up quickly and the butter will start to sizzle, frying the scallops in their own shells. After 1–2 sizzling minutes, flip the scallop meat over without disturbing the shells. Cook for a further 1 minute, until the scallops are cooked through, then remove each shell from the embers. If at any point you think the butter is blackening or bubbling too fiercely before the scallop is cooked, rearrange it in a less hot part of the fire (a little browning is good, though). Set the scallops on plates and tuck in, but remember the shells will be hot!

index

GILL MELLER is a chef, food writer, food stylist and cookery teacher. He has been part of the River Cottage team for over a decade, working closely with Hugh Fearnley-Whittingstall. Gill teaches at the River Cottage Cookery School and internationally, and has written for *The Guardian*, *Waitrose Food Monthly* and *Country Living*. He lives in Dorset with his family. This is his first book.

acknowledgements

There is a dictionary definition of the word 'gather' at the very front of this book. One line reads 'To draw (something or someone) closer to oneself' – it's such a lovely line and in the context of these 'thank yous' feels so right.

It's taken only a year to bring this book together, but it's taken so much more than that to make it feel real for me. I want to thank my family for this. I've been so lucky to live in such a beautiful place, but I've been even luckier to do that with you – Alice, Isla and Coco, thank you.

I owe so much to my friend Andrew Montgomery. I've loved every single day we've spent working together on this book. You've been as much a part of this project as I have. Your pictures are truly beautiful. They have made this book, thank you.

Sarah Lavelle, I can't thank you enough for what you have done. You believed that we could do something great together when we met, a few years ago. You took me with you, and we did it. You have been the perfect publisher.

Thank you to Hugh Fearnley-Whittingstall. Hugh, you've helped me to understand what cooking really means. I will always be grateful for that.

I want to thank Miranda Harvey. I know I've told you already, Miranda, but I can't think of anyone else I would have rather had working with me on this book. You've done such an eloquent thing here. Everything has a voice, thanks to you.

Jude Barratt has done the most wonderful job of editing this book. Thank you, Jude. Your approach has been as sensitive as it has been thorough. Let's do it again.

Thank you to my agent, Antony Topping, who made the complicated appear simple, in the most gentle and careful way.

A massive thank you must also go out to Rob Love, Sally Gale, Steven Lamb, Gelf Alderson, Andy Tyrrell, Will Livingstone and everyone else at River Cottage. Thank you to Helen Lewis, Verity Holliday and everyone at Quadrille who has helped to realize this project. Thank you to Alex Heaton, Chloe Ride, Mark Diacono, Diana Henry, René Redzepi, Olia Hercules, Oliver Gladwin, John Wright, Deborah Robertson, Nikki Duffy Simon Wheeler, Timm Vladimir, Nicole Lehner, Sytch Farm Studios, Crane Cookware, Blunt Roll and to all the amazing ch I've worked with and learned from over the years, and to all the fisherman, farmers, growers and producers that make what w do so special.

Lastly, thank you to my sister and brother, Rose and Patrick, to my Mum and Dad, the people we love to Gather together w the most.

www.gillmeller.com
gill@gillmeller.com
@gill.meller